Flies in the Fan

By

Dr. Karen Hutchins Pirnot

For Charlie
Forever and Always

For those who so courageously search for
Meaning Amongst the Confusion

For Jerri and Letti

For Jan, whose middle name is Courage

FOREWARD:

It is well over one hundred years (1906) since German Psychiatrist Dr. Alois Alzheimer identified a specific type of dementia during an autopsy on one of his patients. By the middle of the twentieth century, both children and adults still secretly commented on someone's Aunt Martha or Uncle Harry that *lived in the attic.* In those conversations, living in the attic was a euphemism for someone having *senile dementia.*

Senile dementia was a term used to describe a Rubik's cube of unidentified cognitive disorders which included both physical and cognitive abnormalities for which significant declines in everyday tasks could be documented.

Since life expectancy was lower in the mid-1950's, incidences of dementia continued to be viewed as oddities that occasionally happened to those less fortunate than we, the majority. However, the increase in population attributable to "baby boomers" has assured that it is not the case in today's population.

One out of every three people 65 and older dies from Alzheimer's disease or a related dementia. Every 66 seconds, someone is diagnosed with a progressive dementia. By 2050, three times as many Americans will be diagnosed with Alzheimer's or another progressive dementia.

Alzheimer's disease currently kills more than breast and prostate cancer combined. It is the sixth leading killer of Americans and yet, it is the only disease in the top ten that has no prevention, no cure, and not even the suggestion of a means of slowing the process of the disease.

In the media, we have brought cancer and Down's syndrome out of the closet. We have attacked cancer straight on with research dollars and we have openly given opportunities to those with disabilities to lead a meaningful and productive life.

It is now time to tackle the most urgent health concern in our nation. The care of those with Alzheimer's disease threatens to stress the healthcare budget to a point of bursting. We need to know when to intervene and when and how to take over the care of a loved one. We need to understand that when a loved one is placed into long-term care, there are those trained and competent, ready to provide an environment of respect and safety to those who have relinquished their roles as husband and wives, brothers and sisters, parents, grandparents and aunts and uncles.

Even though they act differently from the established "norm" of cognitive and behavioral functioning, those afflicted with progressive dementia are not subhuman. They retain their humanity in ways we are not yet educated to appreciate. Just as we had to educate ourselves about racial and gender issues, we now need a more comprehensive understanding of the millions of older citizens who have no choice but to live out a life unscripted, a life in which the known world has both betrayed and dehumanized them.

The story of *Flies in the Fan* is based upon real people in a real Memory Care facility. Characters are derived from residents seen by the author over a ten-year period. All names are fictionalized. The stories are intended to demonstrate how simple acts of kindness and understanding can see loved ones through times of confusion, frustration and fear.

You cannot enter a long-term Memory Care* facility, look around and then walk out the door, heaving a sigh of relief that you have been spared that fate, and then conclude you have educated yourself. You must dare to sit and study. You must dare to believe that the existence in the House of Final Release is honest and real, despite all the cognitive and behavioral evidence of a surreal world so readily observable. You must dare to believe that it is a family you are observing and that there is love and tenderness in every act of care and conversation.

You must see the corporate executive, the accountant, the factory worker, the mother and grandmother, the teacher, the doctor, the food manager and the courageous daily struggles of all of those who, like you, never, ever imagined such an existence.

*Memory Care Unit is the term considered most acceptable for a unit which is *secured*. Secured is the term considered most acceptable for a unit in which the residents are literally locked in. They are secured not because they are dangerous to others. Rather, they are secured so that they are not a danger to themselves.

***

Some would claim that a quick death robs one of everything that makes life worth living. Spouses, brother, sisters, parents, grandchildren and friends are instantly gone and the living are left with the process of letting go. There is a firm belief among some who grieve that if the deceased would only have left life slowly, the living would have time to adjust to what has been lost. But, caregivers of the loved ones residing in memory care units might beg to differ.

Just prior to retirement from her years of paid employment, Charlie's wife knew her husband had a serious problem. It would be some time before she fully understood that Charlie's problems were multidimensional and that he would leave life slowly and in a manner that left everyone who loved him unnerved and challenged to cope with the long and painful good-bye.

Charlie and his wife had stayed the course for over ten years before he went to the House and into a Memory Care Unit. For the first seven years, his wife was his sole caregiver. He then began to attend a local day care group, giving his wife a life-saving respite for a few hours each day. And then, in a single day, Charlie's wife was forced to reformulate the meaning of the wedding vows *"'til death do us part."* For Charlie and his wife, that phrase had always meant living together and sharing life as a couple, as a cohesive unit and under almost any adversity. In a single day, their best-laid plans were shattered, leaving Charlie's wife to struggle with the promise she had made.

***

CHAPTER ONE
THE PROMISE

Take me home. I want to go home right now, Charlie had begged. They were in the hospital and Charlie was in crises.

The day before Charlie had entered the hospital, he was agitated. His wife had taken him out to brunch and he had sat in silence, seemingly unaware of the normalcy surrounding him in the restaurant. He remained anxious and he became delusional. Lately, he had experienced periodic delusional thinking but such episodes had been short-lived. On that day, Charlie's mind did not allow him to find a neural pathway to what had become his *usual* childlike state. They went for a long ride and Charlie's wife put Charlie to bed early that night.

At about three o'clock the following morning, Charlie's wife heard the garage door open. She raced outside while a cold blast of Florida winter smacked her in the face. Charlie was sitting on a lounge chair, wearing only his protective underwear and his Navy hat. The temperature was in the forties outside; it was the coldest night they would experience that year.

Charlie did not respond to his wife's query but she quickly ascertained that her husband was waiting for his ride to his day care group. She asked him to come inside with her but Charlie resisted. She ran back inside the house and grabbed a quilt from the den. She wrapped the quilt around Charlie and struggled to bring his uncooperative body inside where she could get him back to bed. Charlie then slept deeply for about four hours before getting up to wander about the house.

For the past couple of weeks, Charlie's wife had been talking by phone to their primary physician. She was seeing changes in Charlie which needed to be documented. On the morning of the early outside experience, she waited until the physician's office opened and then, she called to report the latest incident. Charlie had previously experienced UTI's (urinary tract infections) which caused alterations in his thinking and behavior, so the doctor requested his wife take him in for a urine sample. They did that and the sample proved to be negative.

Charlie's wife knew what she must now do. She must prepare her husband for the day they both dreaded. She took Charlie to the bathroom. She undressed her husband and took his hand, leading him into the walk-in shower. She was grateful for the newly-remodeled bathroom for she could now walk into the shower to bathe her husband. On this day, she guided him to the seat in the back of the shower stall and Charlie willingly sat for her as she got the showerhead extension, turned on the water and adjusted the temperature. As if he were a fragile newborn, Charlie's wife gently allowed the water to glide over Charlie's head and she then lathered him with soap. Charlie loved the attention. His verbalizations were sparse, but he smiled like an appreciative child whose dream had just come true. As Charlie gazed at his wife, she smiled and cleaned his body and then, she shampooed her husband's hair.

When he could still bathe himself, Charlie almost always forgot to wash his hair. He could not see the hair; thus, it did not exist for him. But, Charlie's wife automatically washed his hair as part of the bathing routine. She massaged his scalp and Charlie closed his eyes in contentment as his wife made ringlets in his thinning, grey hair.

She then picked up the razor and shaved around his cheeks, in all the areas where his beard met skin. The first time she had tried that, Charlie had jerked, causing the razor to nick his skin. But now, he was an appreciative child simply enjoying an act he could no longer perform for himself.

After the bathing routine, Charlie's wife wrapped her husband in towels and sat him on the toilet to attempt to dress him. He fidgeted and she decided to simply put on his protective underwear and his tee shirt. She then took Charlie to the sink and she brushed his teeth. Charlie stared into the mirror. He began to look frightened when he saw his own reflection, so   his wife guided him the few steps back to the bedroom and helped him to lie down on the bed.

Charlie's condition worsened in a few moments time and he became highly agitated and delusional. One moment, he thought he was fifty years back in time as an officer in the Navy. Seconds later, he asked his wife if she had his class notes for his lecture in psychology that day. Seconds later, he asked her where his wife was and then, he headed for the door, to some unknown destination. Unable to verbalize his distress in any other way, he began to grab at his crotch and shake himself violently. His wife took him repeatedly to the bathroom but he was unable to void.

Charlie's wife called their physician and told the nurse she was taking her husband to the emergency room of the hospital which was less than a mile away. She told the physician she thought Charlie was in urinary retention and that he also appeared delusional. The physician wanted Charlie admitted to attempt to stabilize him.

She buckled Charlie in the car and she told her husband they were going to the hospital. Charlie looked frightened so his wife said they would find someone who could help Charlie go to the bathroom.

It took only five minutes to reach the hospital. Charlie's wife parked the car, got out and went to open the passenger door. She unbuckled Charlie and took his hand. She walked her husband into the Emergency Room and continued to hold onto Charlie's hand as if it would be the last walk they would ever take together. She tried to tell herself that Charlie would be treated and she would later take him back home. Her brain attempted to lie to her in a feeble attempt to protect her heart.

Charlie's wife told the nurse that her husband appeared to be in urinary retention. She then quickly followed with the information that Charlie was delusional but that he did not have a psychiatric problem. She offered a small card to the admitting nurse. On the card was written: **My husband is in late stage Alzheimer's Disease.** The nurse smiled and asked Charlie to go with her. Charlie would not let go of his wife's hand and the nurse then told him that, of course, his wife should come as well.

It was quickly ascertained that Charlie's discomfort originated from an over-extended bladder. But, even after the catheterization, Charlie remained highly delusional and combative. He was admitted to the hospital. A catheter and an IV were put in as palliative measures and Charlie immediately pulled them out. This continued for two more days, with Charlie's wife spending the days with Charlie and his wife and a hospital "sitter" spending the nights. On the fourth day, the urologist came in and it was decided that a suprapubic catheter might be preferable. If Charlie tried to pull out the catheter, there might be less tissue damage. The suprapubic catheter was surgically implanted in Charlie's abdomen and as soon as the anesthetic wore off, Charlie went after it.

Medical staff decided that Charlie could not return home to his wife's care. He now required 24/7 supervision by trained staff. Most of the long-term care facilities would not take Charlie due to the severity of his condition and the urgency of placement. But Charlie's wife had visited a facility two weeks earlier, looking for an *eventual* placement should Charlie ever take a turn for the worse. She called the admissions director of the facility in the late afternoon and Charlie was transported by medical van to the facility that evening. His wife held his hand the entire journey and did not let go until he was given medication to help him to sleep.

Charlie's wife had done the roughing in with Charlie over a period of ten years. She had plumbed in trust and wired stability into a man for whom the world was now unknowable. She prayed others could now provide the insulation that prevented Charlie's body and mind from shattering due to the unpredictable vibrations inside.

"With my last breath, I'll exhale my love for you. I hope it's a cold day, so you can see what you meant to me. "
— *Jarod Kintz*

CHAPTER TWO
The House of Final Release

It's a tautology, something true by logic alone. There is no way around it. By simply choosing to live, each one of us gambles with death. There are one hundred and fifty-five residents here in the memory care unit. Like us, not even one of them ever thought it would end like this. In the wildest regions of their fantasies and certainly, never in reality, could this be happening to them. And yet, here they are.

***

On the first day of Charlie's admission to the House, his wife studies the residents. And, she studies for many days after that. She is used to Charlie's peculiar presentation. She does not know the other residents and so, she attempts to learn. The impressions she has on the first day are dramatically altered from those she will have on the day of Charlie's death. She first conceptualizes many residents as robotic but further knowing proves that to be a falsehood. Then, the residents seem childlike and pure, but that is not an adequate working hypothesis either.

Finally, she thinks:

The residents oftentimes seem to mimic the waxing and waning of long-burning candles. An aura of darkness has replaced the light long before the flame is extinguished. Tallow continues to ooze from the candle and drip down the side as if it has purpose and destination. But, the wax is now devoid of intentional form and function and thus, it eventually lays almost inert as it continues to attempt escape from the existing shell which has previously served to preserve the innate ingredients supplying the flame. The wax flow never quite reaches its purpose, for the core composition of the candle is now significantly compromised compared to the exterior structure itself.

Wax trails continues to flow, slipping out and dropping in tandem, one trail hitchhiking on the other to give the impression of meaningful, individual effort. Concerted energy is expended to give the impression that the movement of the tallow trails is routine. But somehow, the tallow trails increasingly mesh with the foundation upon which the candle is set, becoming more and more emeshed with its environment.

No one dares to blow out the candle for no one has been given moral or legal permission to do so. The candle is simply left to burn itself out while others comment on its structure and form. Many tend the candle to keep it burning. Eventually, the wax begins to become accustomed to itself as it lays nearly flat and lifeless. And yet, there is sometimes a flicker of light which continues to struggle to find its environment. Thus, it is the compromised content of the resident candles themselves that supply the foundation for the House. And, each House is different, unique unto itself.

***

On this day, Charlie's wife goes to the wheel chair that has become Charlie's single mode of transportation. Charlie had walked into the Emergency Room of the hospital. He walked with a shuffle, falling on occasion, but he generally got to his intended destination. And now, his legs have failed him. Charlie's wife touches her husband on the shoulder and then, she touches him again, but he seems frozen in time. He turns his head awkwardly and he then emits a smile of recognition. With that small gesture, his wife can proceed with a fair certainly that Charlie knows her on that day.

****

The dining room in the House has vinyl flooring that covers a concrete floor. At any given time, a watchful attendant will be wiping up a spill while gently coaxing a resident not to rise for fear of a fall. You never want to ask what is being extracted from the floor. That's why you wear vinyl gloves when you're wiping up the spill.

Today, Esther has gotten up from her chair and is headed directly toward the dining room door. Noah holds his hands straight in front of Esther and warns *I don't want you to slip on this, Esther. Please go on back to your chair.* In truth, there is no spill where Esther stands. Noah simply wants Esther back in her chair as lunch is about to be served.

Charlie's wife sits down at the table with Charlie and Will. She understands that neither of the men will initiate conversation, so she asks about their day. Will is able to give her a complete sentence which suggests he has some comprehension of what she has asked. *It's good* he replies.

Charlie remains silent so his wife asks if he has gone to physical therapy that day. He looks confused as usual. Sometimes, he says **No**, an answer which may or may not be factual, and sometimes, he will say, *Maybe*. For the most part, Charlie seems content to have his wife converse with Will who is not as advanced in the dementia process as is Charlie. Will can walk without assistance but his gait is awkward and unsteady so he is constantly cued to use his walker.

When Charlie first entered the House, he thought he could walk. After all, Charlie had been walking for almost eighty years and it was somewhat a taken-for-granted activity. But lately, every time Charlie tried to rise from the wheel chair, he fell, sometimes necessitating trips to the emergency room of the local hospital. In the past week, Charlie did seem to gain some realization that he should not rise from the chair unless someone was nearby to assist him. And his wife Is proud of him for that, for having a realization. In truth, she is maybe more relieved than proud, for Charlie no longer remembers he could at one time walk on his own. He watches other residents walk. He has a sense of awe much like that of the nine-month old infant who struggles to understand the concept of an upright position.

Charlie's wife knows that Charlie's *realization* is a lie she tells herself. And the lie is no longer comforting as it was in the beginning and she needs to rid herself of it. In truth, Charlie's Parkinson's has progressed to the point that he no longer has the strength to rise from a sitting position. It is just one of the diseases which has led Charlie to the House in which he now lives.

Charlie is diagnosed with Alzheimer's disease with Lewy Body, Stage Four Parkinson's Disease and Vascular disease with TIA's (Transient Ischemic Attacks) and silent seizures. As if that were not enough, Charlie's genetic inheritance has also besieged him with Barrett's Esophagus and prostate cancer. And, despite her firm intentions to remain Charlie's primary caregiver until the day of his death, Charlie's diseases have played their trump card and he now lives in the House.

The name of Charlie's house is The Woods. That is what is written on the newly-painted white and blue sign outside the front entrance. The House which others call the *facility* is set back into a wooded area. Some people call it a nursing home. Others say it is a place where the living go to die. It's true that there are nurses there to care for the residents but it is a lie to conclude it is a place where people go to die. At least, that is true in Charlie's unit. Those who call Charlie's wing of The Woods *HOME* left living many years ago. For those in the Memory Care Unit of The Woods, it is the House of Final Release.

***

"Carve you name on hearts, not tombstones. A legacy is echoed into the minds of others and the stories they share about you.'
    -Shannon L. Adler

CHAPTER THREE
THE DANCE

The House where Charlie and the others now live is about sixty-five years old, and she, Charlie's wife, is over a decade older than that. In its day, the House was bright and clean and it might even have been considered welcoming on first impression. But, from the beginning, the House was a no-frills kind of place. It was built with perfectly placed concrete blocks and solid studs, without the need for bracing. The House was a lot like those who have occupied the House over decades of time. It was once sturdy and without flaws which call attention to itself. But now, that is no longer the case. The physical House is almost as damaged as the physical residents who dwell within.

When you first open the front door to the House, you see a small sitting area to the left and the receptionist's area is directly in front of you. Brianna always wears a paper mask so she won't be subject to all the germs brought in by the visitors. But, the mask does not protect her from the feelings of apprehension and fear so readily visible on the faces of those who enter.

Brianna is a pleasant woman with caramel latte skin and a beautiful smile. She warms up to you as soon as she knows you're for real. For those who only come to the house out of duty or obligation, Brianna will give a perfunctory but respectful **Hello** and she then gets back to business. If you are a genuine visitor and the pain of your loss is etched on your face, Brianna stops her business to give you an easy smile and a warm, **Hey, hi there. Good to see you.**

Charlie's wife vows that one of these day, she will stop

to find out more about Brianna, and she will. Most visitors are curious about how one would come to work at a House like this. But now, she needs to go left down the hall, and then right.   And then, she needs to knock on the door. The presence of the locked door is enough to give even those with high resolve a case of stomach butterflies. Sometimes, on the faces of new visitors, Charlie's wife can even sense the bile rising from the digestive track. And then, there is that stern look of resolve to keep the acidic repulsion in check so as not to cause personal embarrassment.   Even after months of visits, Charlie's wife still feels a sense of unknowing as she waits for someone to punch in the code to let her in. It is not the occasional visitor kind of stomach butterflies. It is more the accumulation of the pain of loss common to those providing years and years of caring for a loved one who is no longer a participant in life outside of the House.

Whoever is closest to the dining room will be the one to open the doors. There are two doors, held together with a lock. The doors are steel, painted white and battered from years of residents knocking and pounding to get out. Wheel chairs and walkers have done their share of damage as well. If you're tall enough, you can peek through the windows at the top of the door. But, you may not want to do that unless you have some notion of what's on the other side.

Sometimes, it takes two or three knocks, but someone will always come. She – it is usually a she – will always be sure that no one on the other side is close-by, waiting to bolt through the door.   Generally, you hear, *No, Mama, you come with me now,* and then, ever-so-cautiously, the door will open. It is never fully open. Rather it is eased open just enough to let the visitor sneak in quickly.

If she knows the nurse or the aide who has unlocked

the door, Charlie's wife will greet the door opener as she looks to the left, hoping she might find her Charlie in the dining room. Today, Sharma has let her into the memory care wing of the House. Immediately, she hears a man yelling and she surmises it is Frederick. Sharma shrugs and she logically concludes that it is close to the time that Frederick will be given his next shot. No one ignores the shouting man; rather, they respect his right to stay for a time in his own delusion.

Charlie's wife simply accepts Sharma's shrug as verification of her own conclusions about Frederick and she takes a moment to admire Sharma's flawless chocolate skin and her ebony locks of hair. She wishes her own strands of limp, dull, greying hair could suddenly spring to life and pretend they were still in the game rather than be content to be bystanders living a vicarious life.

The large room to the left also serves as an activity room and a music room. It is also the place where parties are held on days which used to be significant to the residents, and still may be to some. On the wall to her right, Charlie's wife glances up at the wide television screen. Oftentimes, Gunsmoke will be playing or perhaps, The Golden Girls. Charlie's favorite is a musical video that features various breeds of puppies romping and exploring the environment with one another. If you look around the room during that video, you can oftentimes see the longing on faces worn thin and fragile with the burning of the flame.

A bank of windows greets the visitor, giving an illusion of freedom of limits between the inside walls of the House and the butterfly garden just out of reach due to the coded box which must be accessed before one can go out to feel the sunshine. Charlie's wife looks around and spots about two dozen men and women, all in various stages of attempting to act out a scene in life they no longer understand. They are actors in a script a playwright has written without realization that the actors can no longer memorize the lines to the scene.

Today, Charlie's wife looks in the dining room and does not see Charlie. She is about to turn to search the hallway when someone says **Charlie is right over there.** Finally, Charlie's wife recognizes the man to whom she has been married for over four decades. Charlie is sitting with a blank look on his face. The wife has failed to recognize her husband because his fifty-year-old beard has been shaved and he is not wearing his eye glasses.

Charlie is sitting at a table with his friend Will. The two men first met at a day care group over a year ago. They now forget that they know one another, so staff re-introduces them daily and they become friends again, and again, and again.

Anita casually tells Charlie's wife there will be a Sweetheart Dance on Valentine's Day and the daily visits are insufficient to prepare Charlie's wife for such a traditionally-intimate event. She knows she is way out of her league. No amount of time in the school of life experience has prepared her to dance with Charlie in his House on Valentine's Day.

*****

On the day of the Valentine's party, Will's wife feels the pressure as well. Charlie's wife knows this because they have talked on the phone. They are becoming friends. Will's wife says her husband can stand up and dance and therefore, she can go through the motions of having a relationship with the strange man who is still known as her husband. Charlie's wife must find a way to create a buffer between the heartache of the man in the wheelchair and the thin lining protecting what is left of her beating heart.

Someone has worked hard to decorate the dining room and some of the residents look forward to having juice and Valentine's cookies. Charlie's wife walks in and spots her husband. He is with Will and his wife. Will's wife looks almost as pale as Charlie's wife, although both have taken care to wear make-up and red shirts.

There will be musical entertainment which is appreciated by the visitors as it gives common ground for conversation while the large, black clock on the wall ticks off minutes of endurance essential to staying the course of the dance party.

And then blessedly, relief makes itself known. One by one, staff members grab the arms of residents who can stand. Residents are carefully pulled from chairs, walkers and wheel chairs. The chair occupants magically rise, supported by the arms of the care provider. Slowly, they begin to move to the urgings of the singer Charlene, a woman with a born penchant for stirring the still and seemingly paralyzed.

Charlene has on a black leotard, with a red tulle shirt which screams out, **I'm too sexy for myself!** She stomps her feet and her voice rises to a sense of urgency, defying anyone in the House to sit idly by while life screams out its sense of pride. Charlene's black arms grasp Leonard and he seems to come alive with a movement which defies his multiple physical and cognitive diagnoses. Leonard grins, and the slight movement turns to a smile which thrusts itself deeply into Leonard's mouth to become laughter and Charlie's wife and Will's wife exchange incredulous glances. They are newbies and they have a lot to learn.

Will's wife stands and goes to Will's walker. Gracefully, she helps her husband to rise and they assume a position which rightfully belongs to accomplished lovers.

They move in harmony as Will forgets about what he has lost and he engages his legs in what is yet available to him.

Leonard cannot stop dancing to save himself. He is possessed with a feeling from long ago and he will not relinquish the motor memory. He dances to exhaustion and when his partner in turquoise medical scrubs eases him back into his wheelchair, Leonard tries to rise again.

Charlie's wife understands what she must do and she rises and grabs Charlie's hands as he sits and smiles at Leonard. She moves him about in the chair and she sees a transformation that eases past pain and finds its way to a tenderness in the here and the now. She chair-dances with Charlie and the more she moves him, the wider his sense of awe. His Parkinson's frozen face finally emerges into a countenance of pure joy and it is tearing her apart because their dances have always been a form of intimacy and now, dancing has taken on a new and uncomfortable meaning.

Charlie's vacant eyes are bright, nearly alive, if only for seconds. He has remembered something and he has transmitted that thought, that feeling and that memory to his wife. It comes like a fiber optic beam, streaking through time and space and it strikes her fragile heart, clean and true. She is brought to her knees with a connection unavailable for years.

The House staff sees distress from others and they begin to chair dance with those left unvisited that day. Will's wife snaps some pictures while Charlie and his wife remain connected in a moment that will surely never again be available in this lifetime. Charlie's wife sucks in the years of tears as Charlie's caregiver and she smiles and allows Charlie the shared memory that her touch has produced from the bowels of his damaged recollections. She struggles to stand until the moment passes and then, the song ends, sparing her sure emotional death.

Charlie and his wife have ended their connection. It occurs to her that the insulation stuffed into the studs of the House was not placed there for the safety of the residents. It is there for her.

***

"I thought about all the things that everyone ever says to each other, and how everyone is going to die, whether it's in a millisecond, or days, or months, or 76.5 years. If you were just born. Everything that's been has to die, which means our lives are like skyscrapers. The smoke rises at different speeds, but they're all on fire, and we're all trapped."
-Jonathan Safran Foer, Extremely Loud and Incredibly Close

Everyone must leave something behind when he dies, my grandfather said. A child or a book or a painting or a house or a wall built or a pair of shoes made. Or a garden planted. Something your hand touched some way so your soul has somewhere to go when you die, and when people look at that tree or that flower you planted, you're there.

It doesn't matter what you do, he said, so long as you change something from the way it was before you touched it into something that's like you after you take your hands away. The difference between the man who just cuts lawns and a real gardener is in the touching, he said. The lawn-cutter might just as well not have been there at all; the gardener will be there a lifetime."
— Ray Bradbury, Fahrenheit 451

CHAPTER FOUR
The Wallboard Within

The studs and insulation of the House are covered with wallboard, sometimes referred to as drywall. Wallboard gives definition to the rooms and it make the structure sturdier and purposeful.

White mineral gypsum is the primary ingredient used to make drywall panels. The mineral is a light-density calcium sulfate rock and is pretty much available every place in the world. The paper which seals in the pulverized and compacted gypsum is generally made from recycled newspaper. Oftentimes, starch is added to the mixture so that the paper can easily adhere to the core mineral. One can easily see that the smooth wallboard interior panels of the house of the final release are common and durable.

Charlie's wife had visited the House only a few times before she correctly concluded that the various staff members serve as the insulation and the protective wallboard for the House. There were none there who were not sturdy. There were none there who could not compact their own needs into small spaces so that the needs of the residents could be served. There were none there who did not need a moment of recognition from time to time as they lovingly tended to those who routinely engaged in the seeming nothingness of their lives.

From the Medical Director to the Administrator, and from the Admissions Director to the Activity Director, the Business Administrator and the Director of Nursing, all were sturdy and purposeful. But, as with the wallboard-making process, it was necessary to add pulp to increase the core tensile strength. The addition of pulp assured that the heavy lengthwise pull would not warp or damage the wallboard under excessive pressure. And so, the Registered Nurses, the Certified Nursing Assistants and the aides routinely shored up and facilitated the decisions of the Administration while physical and occupational therapists attempted to bravely reconstruct the human damage entrusted to them. Without complaint or comment, housekeeping cleaned up the damage and waste. In fact, they were all the Vermiculite particles that prevented physical, emotional and behavioral fires from spreading in the House.

As Charlie's wife is sitting, watching the movement in the dining room, Ben gets up out of his chair. He is one of a few who can move without aides and sometimes, Ben is surprisingly fast and agile. He heads directly to Will's table where Will is enjoying his mid-morning juice and crackers. Like a hungry hawk, Ben swoops up Will's plastic cup of juice. Will immediately protests and before the cup can reach Ben's eager lips, Anita is there to magically take the cup and replace it on the table. But, Ben is not one to be outfoxed. While Anita reaches out her hands to Ben, he again tries to steal the glass of juice. His movement is not graceful and he spills the cup of liquid on the floor as Will lets Ben know in well-chosen profanity that he has the right to stand his ground and that Will has committed a grievous infraction of resident rules.

Charlie is oblivious to the current disruption. He is fascinated with the fish tank only six feet from his face. Henry begins to scream, *No, No, No* as Will lets all of those within hearing distance know he has a magnificent command of four-letter words. Anita gently takes Ben's two hands and she walks backward as she encourages Ben to go forward. Finally, Ben's eyes are engaged with those of Anita's and she smiles and begins to sing softly: *You are my sunshine, my only sunshine. You make me happy when clouds are grey. You never know dear, how much I love you.*

Ben and Anita are now back to where Ben sits for his lunch. As Anita gently encourages Ben toward his seat, still holding his hands, Ben joins Anita in, singing, *Please don't take my sunshine away.*

While Anita positions Ben safely in his chair, Sharma has sped to the scene of the crime, wiping all evidence from the floor. What is no longer seen is not remembered and Will is again smiling and eager for his lunch. For the entire minute of the song, Charlie has not broken his gaze at the fish in the tank but Henry has fallen asleep.

Charlie's wife looks to where Ben is seated. Bonnie has come from nowhere and has tossed a blue linen tablecloth on the table. It is folded and Charlie's wife thinks it is curious indeed, that Bonnie did not spread the cloth on the square dining table. But then, a woman at Ben's table reaches for the cloth and she carefully takes one corner. Ben reaches for another corner and two other women follow the action of the others. It takes a moment but soon, the cloth is laid across the table and Sharma is busy sweeping the creases from the cloth. Charlie's wife watches as, one-by-one, other tables receive cloths and residents carefully do what they can to place the cloth correctly.

She is amazed that such a simple act has soothed the excitable and hungry residents. A tear forms in her right eye as she realizes that any form of function is precious to the residents. They understand what to do at that moment and, for some, it may be the only such moment in their day. They now wait patiently for whatever is coming their way and their ears perk up to the sound of the lunch trays in the hallway.

Henry sleeps and Frank refuses to spread the tablecloth himself. There is no one else at the table. Soon, Bonnie goes to Frank and asks him to help spread the cloth. Frank sits in silence. Bonnie spreads the cloth, smiles and tells Frank that he is in for a treat today. His tray is brought to him and he looks at it and says, *It's shit; it's all shit!* Bonnie hands Frank his fork and he eagerly attacks the plate of food.

When Charlie's tray is brought to the table, his wife knows it is time for her to leave. Charlie does not protest her leaving, as his eyes are now locked on the plate of food and the nearby fish tank becomes yesterday's feature. She kisses Charlie on the forehead and goes to the double steel doors and waits to be released. Anita comes, punches in the code and Charlie's wife goes slowly down the hall, dragging the tragedies and triumphs of the Memory Care unit out the door and into the real world.

***

"Endurance is not just the ability to bear a hard thing, but to turn it into glory."
-William Barcla

CHAPTER FIVE
APPOINTMENTS

The furnishings at the House known formally as The Woods are adequate. When the House was first built, the furnishings may once have been something to stand out and compliment the House. But now, the appointments are in their proper places, in the background so that the residents take their rightful places of prominence.

All the spouses and children of residents in the House looked at many such places before a decision was made to place a loved one in permanent care. Most of those who fail to see inside the house of the final release are caught up in the dazzling chandeliers and the hype of the latest *life enrichment* techniques at other such places. The trappings impress those with guilty feeling about the placement of a loved one.

But the families of those in the House have gone inside and have dared to feel the life their loved ones will experience. Everything inside is *serviceable*. Residents can scuff up the walls and pee on the floor. They can yell frustrations at the walls and curse at the wheel chair that has just violated your foot space. As a resident, you can ask and you will be heard. You can have wonderful, delusional living moments and the staff will jump right in and ride the pleasant waves of your compromised but imaginative mind while, all the time, carefully keeping you safe from harm.

Staff has periodically been teased with the thoughts of a *remodel* by *corporate*. But basically, they are content to simply keep the House sanitary and comfortable. For staff, the residents serve as both the foundation of the structure and the appointments therein. That arrangement makes those who live within the House tend to the truly important process of respectfully releasing from life. The staff couldn't tell you what period of furnishings are in the House, but they can tell you the names of the individual residents.

Sharma knows that Charlie must have his liquids thickened and Anita knows when Grandma has gotten up from her chair and is a risk to fall. Beth knows that when Henry screams, he can be soothed with familiar phrases and Lettie knows that when the very dignified Anderson begins to lose control, he can have his dose of antipsychotic a few minutes early. It is all done so smoothly, simply because the physical appointments are insignificant and the staff knows the names of those dwelling in the House.

The House has taken on its presence because it has been lived in and *used*. When Alice allows the shower to run long after she has finished her lunch, Ellie will be in her room taking care of the flood effects. When Will flushes his Depends down the toilet, Curt will be handy with a mop and a plunger to keep the fixture functioning yet another day. When Esther begins to accuse men with blank stares of violating her in one of her three marriages, Bonnie will quickly ask her about her *medical career*, that of being married to a physician. And, when Ben reaches for food belonging to someone else, Anita will be there to guide him to a place of safety to the strains of *You are my sunshine, my only sunshine.*

Eventually, the caring actions of those employed at the House has taken the place of pleasing appointments at the House. Eventually, there may be a remodel, an *updating*, so to speak. However, the new appointments will be totally ignored by the residents. But, a remodel may be of importance to visitors who cannot see the splendor and wealth of the existing appointments.

***

No pain that we suffer, no trial that we experience is wasted in ministers to our education, to the development of such qualities as patience, faith, fortitude and humility. All that we suffer and all that we endure, especially when we endure it patiently, builds up our characters, purifies our hearts, expands our souls and makes us more tender and charitable, more worthy to be called the children of God... and it is through sorrow and suffering, toil and tribulation, that we gain the education that we come here to acquire.
   -Orson F. Whitney

CHAPTER SIX
THE DAYS

Today, it is Chuck who opens the locked doors for Charlie's wife. He smiles and immediately tells her that Charlie is taking a nap in his bed. And so, she considers the dining room where an entertainer is setting up to sing. She spots Will and goes to him.

Charlie's wife is happy that Will has recognized her. She and Will's wife have an agreement. They now go to the House on alternate days and they always stop to see their own husband as well as the husband of the other. That way, both Will and Charlie have a visitor each day. The schedule relieves each wife of ongoing feelings of stress from the letting go process.

Will and his new friend Charlie's wife chat for some time about the performer who is almost ready to sing. Charlie has told his wife in the past that the singer has a lovely voice and she also has a pleasant whistle. Charlie has further conveyed to his wife that he has little tolerance for whistlers but that Cassie is very pleasant to his ears. When Charlie's wife conveys Charlie's remark to Will, he thinks for a moment and then says he doesn't whistle.

When Cassie begins to sing, Charlie's wife can see how the singing soothes and pleases the residents of the House. Anita and Sharma get up and begin to dance to the rhythm of Cassie's songs. Then, Judd begins to follow Sharma around. He does not dance; rather he is interested in Sharma's movements.

Charlie's wife looks around and sees that Will is totally engaged in Cassie's performance but that Esther and Barbara are staring at her. She understands that the stares mean they also wish to have company. She goes to their table and greets the two women warmly.

There is a third woman there who remains silent. Immediately, Esther begins to tell about how she acquired the diamond ring on her right ring finger. A favorite uncle gave it to her at her high school graduation and he is both a physician and a pharmacist. Charlie's wife thinks that the uncle is a busy man indeed. She tells Esther that the uncle must love her very much. And then, Barbara becomes very serious about needing to get married. She has had a rather major stroke and movement in her right arm and leg are severely limited. She is wearing a blue fabric brace on her right hand. She is confined to a wheel chair and has learned to adapt well to her new mode of transportation.

Both Esther and Barbara compete for the attention of Charlie's wife and she attempts to accommodate to them both while also tuning in to the pleasant entertainment in the dining room. Soon, Beth comes into the dining room wheeling Charlie and she spots his wife. She brings Charlie over to the table where his wife is sitting.

Charlie smiles and reaches out his left hand to his wife and she takes it in her own. Charlie's right hand used to caress his wife routinely but it now curls and fails to cooperate in assisting its owner. Charlie's wife is simply grateful that once again, her husband sees and acknowledges her. Because Charlie does not use her name, she is unsure that he understands their long, intense connection. But, he knows her face, and that is good enough for today.

Charlie's interest goes to the performer and Esther and Barbara again solicit the attention of Charlie's wife. Esther now begins a monologue about having been a buyer for her uncle's department store. She relates how she can pick out a beautiful dress at no cost to her. The delusions are rambling but the vocabulary is sophisticated Charlie's wife can see how Esther is able keep the attention of almost anyone with her various animated stories.

Barbara is not content to sit back and she asks Charlie's wife if Frank might be a suitable man to marry. Frank is sitting two feet away but he is oblivious to the conversation. An aide has brought him a sandwich and juice as he elected to sleep through lunch. No one in the room thinks twice about Frank's special treat. It is a given that some people eat at one time of the day and others, at another time.

Esther comments that she gets her treats at bedtime. Staff will oftentimes bring small cups of pudding that contain medication. Most of the resident of the House look forward to the vanilla pudding treat. Others will simply swallow a pill.

Suddenly, Esther points to Connor, a man who continually paces the floor. He stops in a predetermined spot, looks around and then, lifts his right foot and he again begins to pace. Esther explains to Charlie's wife that Connor is a security guard and that he checks the doors to make sure no one can get in. Esther also relates that Connor is sometimes in her room watching over her at night but that he *never does anything but look.* Charlie's wife understands that Connor suffered a TBI (Traumatic Brain Injury) in an automobile accident some time back and that the pacing is an obsession he will probably have the rest of his life. Connor is the youngest in the House. He does not speak. He simply paces. If doors are left unlocked, Connor will pace himself right out into a line of traffic.

Charlie's wife asks if the presence of Connor makes Esther feel safe and, simultaneously, Esther and Barbara nod and say *yes!* Charlie's wife is continually amazed at how the delusional thinking of many of the residents fits into a schema that truly accommodates to the individual needs of the residents.

Cassie is now singing "Unchained Melody" and Charlie's wife joins in. Charlie turns to her and she moves his wheel chair a bit closer to her. Charlie locks his eyes with those of his wife and they have a special moment which is abruptly ended when Barbara taps her arm and asks if she should marry Frank. Esther comments to Barbara that she should take her time and think about the *right man to marry.* Charlie's wife wonders if the intimate connection with her husband has been painful for the two women and she directs attention to them as they begin to plan their weddings.

Barbara takes great effort to move her chair in front of and to the side of Frank's chair. She bends down and retrieves two pieces of bread crust from the floor and places them on the table next to Frank's drink cup. Frank has a sullen look. He takes note of the bread crusts and pushes them aside. Barbara returns to her place to the right side of Esther. Many messages are conveyed without the need for speech.

Esther confides she has been married two times and that they were both *shits*. Charlie's wife remembers that only two days ago, Esther confided she had been married three times. Barbara goes along with the mood Esther has set, telling Charlie's wife that her husband left her. Her eyes begin to tear so Charlie's wife takes Barbara's hands and begins to sing along with Cassie. "Oh Susanna" is Cassie's song now and many residents have joined in the singing. Sharma and Anita are having a blast adapting to the meter of the song and residents are clapping to the beat. Charlie has forgotten about his wife and his attention is solely fixed on Cassie.

Chuck has been tending to residents in the room. He gives hugs and settles those who are restless. One never knows what feelings a specific song might trigger in those who reside in the House. After a while, he comes to sit with Charlie's wife. She comments on how attentive he is and asks him how he first made the decision to work in the house of the final release. ***My heart has always been there, helping people,*** he says. And, Charlie's wife believes it because she has seen it firsthand. Chuck takes online courses at night. He wants to be able to administer more fully to those who have left those abilities behind. He loves his work he says, ***but there may be other ways I can help.***

While Esther and Barbara talk about Esther's ring and Barbara's wedding, Sharma and Anita continue to entertain with nonstop dance moves. Judd continues to follow Sharma like an attentive detective. He is particularly interested in her rhythmic posterior. Connor paces directly in front of the dancers and Sharma attempts to take his hands. He stares at her and clenches his hands to his chest. Then, he raises his right foot and begins to pace in another direction. Charlie's wife believes the dancers must be exhausted by now and yet, they continue. And then, she thinks back to fifty and sixty years ago when she had non-stop energy as well.

Suddenly, the third woman at the table is directly in front of Charlie's wife. She asks to please have her red sweater fastened. She has started the snapping wrong and there is one extra snap left on the left side of the sweater. Barbara immediately sets out to figure out the problem, as she correctly ascertains that something is askew. Charlie's wife knows the process has been started incorrectly but she refrains from commenting. Both Esther and Barbara are highly invested in solving the snap issue for the woman in the red sweater.

Finally, Charlie's wife unsnaps the sweater and she positions it correctly, securing the snaps from top to bottom. She asks the woman her name and the childlike voice answers, *I don't know* and so Charlie's wife says she will call her the beautiful woman in the bright red sweater. The woman is very pleased and she returns to her seat.

Charlie's wife ponders what has just occurred. Apparently, the woman in the red sweater had been studying her and the woman thought Charlie's wife possessed the competency to handle her problems. She had noticed this same adaptive trait in others who needed help. Like small puppies, the residents had an uncanny means of asking for assistance from those they perceived as having solutions to their problems. Charlie's wife thinks to herself that since most of the residents have some form of progressive dementia and had previously handled their own needs without assistance, it was truly an adaptive trait to be able to seek help when their own cognitive and behavioral skills betrayed them.

Charlie abruptly turns and attends to his wife. It is as if he has totally forgotten about her presence for a while. His wife takes his right hand in hers and she attempts to unfold the fingers which are curled into a fist. She knows the Parkinson's worsens almost by the day now and she silently asks any present entity how much more a human body can endure.

Esther begs attention from Charlie as she begins to talk about how she has just gotten her hair washed and colored. Charlie's wife comments on how lovely her hair looks and then, the fingernails are presented for inspection. Esther explains that someone just comes and sits outside and does your nails.

Charlie's wife comments that her nails look beautiful and Barbara's nails also look lovely. The nails of the ring fingers on the right hands of both women are colored with a blue polish while the other nine nails are all a rather bright shade of pink.

Charlie's wife is curious and she asks about the rebel nail. Neither Esther nor Barbara has a ready answer and finally, Esther says *it is to remind us of something.* When Charlie's wife then does the obvious follow up about the reminder, Barbara says *I forgot.*

As Cassie is singing her final song, Chuck comes to Barbara and asks if he might remove her hand brace. He asks again if he has permission to do so and Barbara nods. Chuck reminds Barbara that they cannot leave the brace on for too long. Charlie's wife takes that moment to give Charlie a hug and a kiss. The three women at the table are preoccupied with the removal of the hand brace and they will not notice the moment of intimacy.

When the brace is removed, Chuck gently massages the fingers and comments to Barbara on how straight the fingers are getting. Barbara looks confused but then, she smiles. There seems to be a disconnection between the spoken word and the comprehension of that word. The tone of Chuck's comments has conveyed a good feeling. And, Barbara has reciprocated as best she can to what she did not comprehend.

On her way, out of the dining area, Charlie's wife looks for Will, but he has gone back to his room. He may need a change of undergarments – that is, if he has not gone commando that day.

Cassie is packing up her guitar and Charlie's wife has said her good-byes to those she knows. She also says good-bye to those who look at her with some type of faint recognition. She looks at the residents of the House and she fully understands on that particular day, the House is really a home for them. They are family.

***

"I used many times to touch my own chest and feel, under its asthmatic quiver, the engine of the heart and lungs and blood I possessed. Not magical power, but real power. The power simply to go on, the power to endure, that is power enough, but I felt I had also the power to create, to add, to delight, to amaze and to transform."
     -Stephen Fry

CHAPTER SEVEN
THE CARED FOR

In many similar facilities, the cared for are not necessarily the cared about. Even though basic needs are met, many residents of the House have no one to visit or care about them. But, in this House, the residents are both cared for and cared about.

Ann and Clara come together down the hallway and stop in front of the nurses' desk. They are holding hands and are like young school girls, planning their day, secure in their friendship with one another. They smile and tell the nurse *We love you, we love you so much.* Nurse Lettie is typing notes on the computer, but she takes the time to stop and smile at the women. Then, she rises from her seat and she goes to Ann and Clara, giving each of them a generous hug, saying *And, I love you too.* It is a small gesture and yet, it might make or break the day of a resident. Many sit in wheel chairs or stand with walkers. They watch the nurses and the CNA's and they wait for an occasional smile. They are among some of the most patient people Charlie's wife has ever seen.

Henry's protective underwear needs a change. It is highly noticeable as it sags well below the crotch of Henry's thin, grey leisure pants. Lettie gently takes his hand and leads him back to his room where he will be cleaned and soothed and made presentable. She does this not for the approval of the hypothetical family that never comes to visit. She does it simply because if it the right thing to do.

Will has come out of his room and is shuffling down the hallway with a sock and slipper on his left foot. He has only a sock on the right foot and Beth is afraid Will might fall because of an uneven shuffle. She has Will stop and sit on the seat of his walker. She quickly secures the walker brakes while saying she will be back momentarily. *Stay there, Willie,* she calls out as she races to Will's room and retrieves his other slipper from the trash can.

Beth hurries back to where Will has remained seated, carefully brushing off the slipper as she scurries. Will is oblivious to his unorthodox dress code and when Beth places the slipper on his foot, he is confused. But, unlike other times, he does not spew forth his extensive *f-word vocabulary* and Beth is relieved that for the moment, she has made it less likely that Will has a tumble as he proceeds toward the dining room for the day's entertainment. It is only a minor interruption in Will's eventual goal and he will forget it before he arrives at the door of the dining room. But, while Beth has visited Will's room to retrieve the slipper, she sees that the bathroom is again flooded and she puts in a call to housekeeping as she races down the hall saying *No, Thomas, don't stand up. You need help, Thomas.* But, Thomas falls anyway, and the medical director is called because this time,

Thomas has hit his head on the floor and will need to go to the emergency room to have an examination to be sure Thomas does not have a concussion. Before transport arrives, Thomas' sister will be notified of the fall. It is but one of five *incident reports* that Jerri has written up on that day. And, when Thomas' sister is notified, Jerri understands she will listen patiently while the sister again criticizes the House for not paying proper attention to Thomas.

Thomas' nurse Jerri is also Charlie's nurse. And, Charlie's wife has just appeared at the nursing station to talk with Jerri. The nurse finishes typing the incident report so that important details will not be forgotten and she then turns

to Charlie's wife who has waited patiently, knowing she will be addressed shortly.

Soon, it is her turn, As Charlie's wife talks with her husband's nurse Jerri about a sore that has recently developed on Charlie's heal, she observes these tiny moments of caring and she understands they are nothing compared to the overall complexity of the day. Charlie's wife comes at many different times during the week and it is always the same; the cared for are also the cared about at this House. Jerri explains to Charlie's wife how the skin breaks down the same as other body organs. Staff always examines the residents for such breakdowns and provides treatment in the early stages. It is only on rare occasions that a patient will notice her/his own complications.

As she enters the dining room and looks about for Charlie, Charlie's wife spots her husband sitting at a table with his *girlfriend*. Esther has made it known to all who will listen that she and Charlie will soon marry and that her new boyfriend is, indeed, a highly moral man. Two weeks ago, staff made Charlie's wife aware that Esther had fixated on Charlie as she had done with dozens of men since coming to the House two years ago. Staff has told Esther that Charlie is married but that does not resound as a real fact in Esther's delusional reality.

Esther stands protectively at Charlie's right side and she gently strokes his right hand. Like Charlie's wife, Esther has noticed the increased tremor in Charlie's right hand and as she strokes the arm, Charlie's tremor becomes less intense. The gesture not only seems to relax Charlie's arm; it also brings great joy to Esther's face.

Although an issue could be made about relationship *boundaries,* Charlie's wife takes the time to study the interaction. Charlie is so obviously cared *about* by Esther that traditional boundaries seem irrelevant. Charlie is slumped to the right and does not seem reactive to Esther's consoling attempts one way or another.

The obvious *solution* to the relationship issue is for Charlie's wife to disallow any notion of competition. She sits at the table and immediately comments on Esther's lovely dress. Esther smiles and she sits while commenting that it is a **Dior dress.** Esther then begins a lengthy monologue about how the dress was especially made for her and she points out the features of the dress, standing and then sitting again to continue her highly-scripted speech as Charlie continues to stare at his wife. Charlie's wife notices that Esther's vocabulary is sophisticated and her verbalizations are fluid, despite the cognitive complications of her dementia. In fact, Esther presents to Charlie's wife as a bright and socially gregarious woman who was probably used to being validated in her life prior to residing in the House.

Charlie then brings a smile of recognition to his lips and his wife goes to him and gives him a generous hug while Esther continues her story. Charlie's arm is stroked by his wife and she notices that he is basically non-reactive to the touch. But the touching does seem to lessen the tremor.

When Esther has finished her monologue about the worn and lifeless dress she is wearing, Charlie's wife then tells Esther she is a good *friend* to the family and that she and Charlie's *family* are delighted that he has such a good *friend* to help him when she is not available.

Esther ponders the statements uttered by Charlie's wife and then, she reaches out to again caress and rub Charlie's arm while her eyes remain locked on Charlie's wife. Charlie's wife asks her husband if the rubbing *feels okay,* and Charlie responds, *I guess.* Esther then mentions that she comes from a medical family and Charlie's wife replies that Esther does, indeed, *have some notion about how to comfort others.*

Ever-so-gently, the roles of the principles in Esther's delusion are shifting while she stands her ground behaviorally. Charlie's wife shows her husband the latest photos of their grandchildren from last night's baseball game. She shows the pictures to Esther and Esther asks the names of the children. Charlie is unsure and so his wife provides the answer. Esther removes her hand from Charlie's right arm and she begins to talk about her three husbands, telling Charlie's wife that *One of them died and he was okay but two of them were real basket cases.*

While Esther goes on about her failed marriages, Charlie's wife nods and reflects on her knowledge that Esther no longer has visitors of her own. Esther is a woman who can adapt and she has not attempted to merge her own lonely feelings with those of residents. Once that is understood, there is no violation of boundaries as Esther's actions are fully reasonable.

Suddenly, Tom walks by and Esther points to him and emphatically tells Charlie's wife that he is one of her ex-husbands and that he is certainly not worth spending time on. Charlie's wife understands that Esther may be trying to reformulate her own delusion.

Charlie's wife nods and Esther then focuses on Connor who is again pacing the dining room. Esther sees Connor and she smiles as Charlie's wife comments on how good *security* is at the House in which both Charlie and Esther reside. Esther has several events in her mind and she appears able to play them at will. Charlie's wife admires Esther's ability to make her own life meaningful and eventful, simply by using the environment at hand.

Over a two-week period, the two women have come to an unspoken agreement. While Charlie's wife is visiting, Esther will respect her position. She and Charlie's wife will be friends in conversation. When Charlie's wife is not present at the House, Charlie may receive comfort from the woman from the medical family.

For some reason, Charlie's wife tunes in to conversation from a nearby table where two visitors sit, talking with one another. She does not recognize the visitors but she understands the words *demented* and *ignorant of their own problems.* The words are like an abrasive drag of skin on the sidewalk. She is angry as she realizes that the person who is *visited* sits at the table as well. He is mute but his eyes are focused and his jaw is clenched as he murmurs *no, no, no, no, no*. Louie remains otherwise silent as the two visitors bid him good-bye and they take their relieved, *obligatory visit* faces out to the hallway to be let out of the secured, battered doors.

Ten minutes after the two visitors leave and return to their world, beverages are served. Louie is agitated waiting for the aide to serve him. He needs the juice to make things right. His six foot, two-inch frame suddenly bolts upright and heads with remarkable agility and purpose to Henry's table.
Henry has already sipped his juice and he will finish the rest in due time. But, Louie bolts to Henry's table with his arms out as Anita shouts *No, Louie, no! Stop that, Louis!!* She then realizes she has spoken impulsively and she says *Oh,*

Louie, I'm so sorry we missed you. You must be thirsty after your visit. As Louie physically attempts to slap at Anita, she takes Louie's left hand and murmurs softly to him as she escorts him back to his table. Sharma quickly gets a glass of juice for Louie. They understand that Louie was, indeed, very thirsty on that day. He was thirsty to be cared *about* and it had not come his way.

Anita and Sharma do not have to know the content of the harm. Louie and the others show the content with their feelings and their behaviors. It is what is available. The recipients of anger at the House are not generally those who provoked the anger. Rather, the anger comes from things remembered and often, from just the pure frustration of the situation. Those possessing the anger must act it out with the means left to them.

Louie sits sipping his juice and the tension in his face releases. Charlie's wife cannot help but think what a proud man sits at that table. Louie is a handsome man in his eighties. He has thick, greying hair and he sits upright, just as he had for forty-eight years at his executive desk as the president of a small insurance firm. Louie worked at a time when secretaries and others routinely brought him coffee. And, they never forgot.

Anita sits with Louie for three minutes, a luxury duration of time in the House. She takes the anger meant for others and she gives *caring about* in return. She asks if Louie has his **work done for the day** and Louie nods and says he **needs to sign a couple more papers.** He will be good for the rest of the night now.

As she leaves that day, Charlie's wife has a clearer comprehension about those in the House. Many have dementia but they are not demented and certainly not stupid. They are not foolish or dull and they are certainly not ignorant. They may be unaware of the environment known to their visitors but they are highly aware of what transpires in their House. They take what is available and they create each day as it comes. For some, the day is replayed time after time after time and they become accomplished in their reactions. For others, the day is new and they must try to adapt to new misfiring in their brain, a misfiring that would challenge and buckle the emotional reserves of those who visit the House.

***

If for a while, the harder you try, the harder it gets, take heart. So it has been with the best people who ever lived.
-Jeffrey R. Holland

CHAPTER EIGHT
THE MUSIC

On this day, a nurse pushes in the door code to let Charlie's wife into the memory care unit. Charlie's nurse Jerri immediately says that Charlie has had a rough morning. In the early morning, Charlie went into urinary retention again. Jerri explains that she had to put in a new catheter. Jerri's actions physically hurt Charlie but he tried to be brave.

Jerri says Charlie is growing very weak and he uttered the word *ouch* several times during the procedure. Then, at the end of the procedure, Charlie had said *Thank you*. Charlie's nurse stresses that Charlie is **such** *a sweet man.* Jerri betrays her usually noncommittal facial expression as she smiles. Her kind words tend to ease the tension visible on the face of Charlie's wife. Jerri says that Charlie is in bed and his lunch must be taken later as he has been given medication for his pain.

Charlie's wife feels such gratitude for Charlie's nurse who, only three short months ago did not know Charlie. The two caregivers stand to talk about the care meeting which took place less than a week ago. At that meeting, it was agreed that Charlie was making no progress in physical therapy. In fact, he seemed to be failing at a rather rapid rate. Charlie's wife had agreed that it was now time to discontinue physical therapy and to call in hospice. Charlie would be made comfortable while he struggled to release himself from his internal trappings. Charlie's wife fights off a tear as she turns to leave. She catches the glint of moisture in Jerri's eyes as she stifles a gasp to maintain her own composure.

As she walks down the hallway, Charlie's wife is sad she will not be able to feed him today. Lately, she has come during the noon meal to feed her husband. Charlie's right hand is now clenched into a tight fist and the left hand has such a tremor that the hands are pretty much useless in everyday functioning. So today, there will be no meal. There may be no way for Charlie's wife to help him on this day and she feels the heavy weight of helplessness as she enters Charlie's room.

Charlie is sound asleep. The head of his bed is raised. His breathing is steady but somewhat shallow. His mouth is open as if he is struggling to get every ounce of oxygen from the surrounding air into his frail body. His wife touches him tenderly across his forehead and his cheeks but he does not stir. She pulls up Charlie's wheel chair and sits for a few moments and then, she decides she will take her need to care for Charlie to others who may not have *someone* today.

In the hall, Charlie's wife meets Barbara. She stops and notices that Barbara has one shoe on her lap. It is the shoe containing the leg brace that Barbara wears on her right leg in addition to the hand brace she wears on her right hand. When Charlie's wife asks if the brace should be on Barbara's leg, Barbara says **The commotion of it all is what you can't get unless you really want it.** Charlie's wife immediately understands that the words are just not there for Barbara to use today. So, Charlie's wife asks if she might take Barbara up the hallway to the dining room as lunch is about to be served. Barbara continues her word salad response but Charlie's wife notices she is shaking her head. Perhaps, Barbara wants to take herself to the dining room when she is good and ready. So, Charlie's wife says she will see Barbara shortly and Barbara smiles. The communication has been good because it has been true to Barbara's needs.

At the dining room door, Charlie's wife stops to look around the room. She is looking to see if Will has made it there for lunch. He has not, but she spots Esther who waves to her. She goes to the table where Esther sits with another woman. It is a woman Charlie's wife has noticed before. Esther and Charlie's wife exchange conversation. As Connor goes by pacing, Esther says to Charlie's wife that *He is my son. Just look behind you and you will see my son.* Two days ago, Connor had been the security guard and now, he was in the role of Esther's son. Charlie's wife marveled that Esther had such a rich and meaningful array of role players in her daily life.

Esther is also a proper and polite lady and she feels it necessary to introduce her table mate. *She sings; she sings really nice,* says Esther as she smiles at the other woman. Charlie's wife turns to the woman and the woman says *I will sing.* She immediately begins singing:

> *I'll be loving you, always*
> *With a love that's true, always.*
> *When the things you've planned*
> *Need a helping hand*
> *I will understand... ... ...always, always.*
>
> *Days may not be fair, always,*
> *That's when I'll be there, always,*
> *Not for... ...Not for... ...*
> And, the woman stops and looks at Charlie's wife.

There is fear in her eyes. Charlie's wife takes a deep breath and sings,

> *Not for just an hour,*
> And the woman then sings,
> *Not for just a day,*

And, together, they sing,
Not for just a year... ....but, always.

The woman and Charlie's wife sing in unison and they both have tears in their eyes. They both have memories that are private but now, their pain is public and neither is ashamed to bear it.

What is your name? Charlie's wife asks.
Jean, the woman says.
That was my mother's name, Charlie's wife says. *She was a concert pianist.*
Yes. And I was a singer. The singer named Jean reaches out her hands and Charlie's wife takes them in hers.

I told you she was a good singer Esther says. And, Charlie's wife excuses herself because the moment is simply way too deep and intense for her to stay in it.

The lyrics to the song sung by Jean were written by Irving Berlin in 1925. In his 60-year career, Berlin would write the lyrics to over 15,000 songs. It was incredible that his song *Always* would be the one to bring together two strangers in separate but shared pain almost one hundred years after the song was written.

Charlie's wife wants to visit with others but she cannot bring herself to move around the dining room. Instead, she again heads down the hallway to see if her husband has awakened. She enters his room and he is in the same position, laying sound asleep, with his mouth open. She sits in the chair and she begins to sing:
Days may not be fair, always,
Charlie's mouth closes.
That's when I'll be there, always,

Charlie's eyes began to move under his closed eyelids.

Not for just an hour,
Not for just a day,
Not for just a year, but always.

Charlie's wife gets up and leans over to kiss her husband on his forehead. There is a small tear escaping from the corner of Charlie's right eye. His wife brushes it away and brings the moisture of the tear to her lips.
And then, she leaves.

In the hallway, Charlie's wife thinks to check on Will. She goes to his room. Will is just putting on his glasses. Charlie's wife tells Will he should go to the dining room for lunch and Will asks **Where's that?** Charlie's wife says she will walk with him down the hall to the dining room. Her throat is so filled with memories that she cannot formulate a question or remark to make the walk less awkward. When they enter the dining room, she points Will toward his table and he said **Thanks.**

She goes to the locked doors and there is the lady in the red sweater asking to leave with her. Charlie's wife asks an aide what the lady's name is and then, she says, *I'm sorry,* *Addy, I cannot take you today. Maybe next time.* The aide presses in the door code. Addy touches the right shoulder of Charlie's wife and then, she takes the hand of the aide and goes into the dining room.

Irving Berlin and his family left their native Russia when Irving was but five years old. It is said that the only recollection he has of having lived in Russia was one of lying in a ditch by the side of the road, watching his house burn to the ground.

***

She pulls into the driveway of the home that such a short time ago had been occupied by Charlie and her. Charlie's wife sits in the car, feeling numb and helpless. She looks around, fully expecting to see her house burning to the ground.

***

Life is not a PG feel-good movie. Real life often ends badly. Literature tries to document this reality, while showing us it is still possible for us to endure nobly."
  -Matthew Quick

CHAPTER NINE
Will's Wife

She is petite and always beautifully groomed. One would conclude that Will's wife shops only in the very best stores. In truth, she is a bargain hunter and her territory has no limits.

When Will and his wife left New Jersey to retire in Florida, Will had held an important position as a distributer. His wife worked in finance and she was appalled when she discovered her husband had invested with a man who talked the talk and walked the walk but generally failed to produce. Even though the scammer is now incarcerated, a good portion of the couple's retirement income had already been lost before the retirement even got off the ground. Sadly, the story of Will and his wife is more common than uncommon.

Like Charlie, Will is a clever man and his wife did not understand how compromised her husband was in the early stages of his disease. Clever and creative victims with progressive dementia can hide their symptoms for the entire balance of the **mild** stage of the disease. And yet, it is in the early stages of the disease that devastating decisions are made, decisions which affect health, retirement and physical comforts.

And so, Will's wife has learned to adapt. She and Will left their spacious, two story home in New Jersey and they adapted to a six hundred square foot condominium on the Gulf of Mexico. Creative as she was, Will's wife figured that if should could look upon paradise daily, she could do without the creature comforts that many retirees take for granted.

Will's wife decided early on that their available funds would be used to invest in two properties, one in which they would live and another which would be rented out for monthly income. In addition to their two monthly Social Security checks, the rental income would allow them to keep up with the yearly cost of living. They would need to be frugal, but it could be done.

When you meet Will's wife for the first time, you may fail to take away from the meeting how very resourceful the woman is. Her face is lined from years of cherishing the sun but her mischievous eyes reveal an intellect that is sometimes elusive but always present. She looks as if she could **cut loose**, but her frivolous nature is displayed only to family and close friends.

On this day, Will's wife goes in to shower her husband. Will has not allowed staff to shower him and without a shower, Will's wife will not visit. And so, she showers him and he enjoys the attention. As he is being dried off, Will smiles and says, *so, how about some sex then!*

Will's wife chokes on her own gasp of air. It has been a long, long time since she and her husband have been intimate. She has parented him for too many years now and to have intercourse would be tantamount to engaging in incest in her mind. Most of the husbands and wives in the house of final release have those feelings. Some are afraid of any kind of intimacy because they are strangers to the ones they wed long ago. But there are others who will take intimacy any way it is presented.

Will's wife distracts him and he soon forgets about having sex. He also forgets where his room is and at times, he stares at his wife, trying to find her as well. It is all simply part of the day for Will's wife.

Will's wife checks her husband's hamper for clothing to take home. Even though staff will do the laundry, Will's wife does his laundry because if she does only her own, it is not even a full wash load. She watches how she uses electricity and she plans on how to save on the water bill. Since Will's admission to the House, his wife has had to talk almost daily to an elder law attorney about how to keep herself out of the proverbial poorhouse.

Fortunately, in some states, there are laws that specify that the illness of one spouse cannot *impoverish* the other spouse. If criteria are met, much of the couple's income can be protected for the non-ill spouse so that those funds are not depleted simply in the care of the ill spouse. And now, Will's wife spends hours gathering information sot her case can be considered.

Well-meaning friends tell Will's wife she should have gotten long-term care insurance. Others tell her they have funds set aside so that should one of them become ill, the other spouse has adequate funds for their care. Will's wife thinks to herself that those friends may be simply spitting at the wind as most insurance is only partial payment for those in a memory-care unit these days. As for those who have money set aside, well, it may last them a few months at best. Unless friends and family are also caregivers, there is little comprehension of how a devastating, long-term illness can eat up one's dreams and financial resources.

And so, Will's wife watches her pennies. She will luncheon with friends, always checking the cost of the meal and considering that she might take home *leftovers* for dinner. She does not consider herself poor; rather she considers herself financially challenged as do many spouses of those in the House.

On this particular day, Will has made it safely to the dining room where he spots Charlie. They communicate in their own way while Will's wife looks about for Charlie's wife.

When the women spot one another, they greet one another like childhood friends when, indeed, they have known one another only three months. They first met in a day care support group and then, Will entered the House. Within a month, Charlie was sent there as well.

The two wives agree to meet at a nearby restaurant. Will's wife orders from the pre-lunch snack menu while Charlie's wife orders a sandwich, half of which can be taken home. Over their meal, the women wonder how they got to riding down this unpredictable road and both conclude that Fate stepped in and sent them down the muddy, pock-marked road when they thought they were already secure on blacktop.

***

"I liked being a person. I wanted to keep at it."
John Green, The Fault in Our Stars

CHAPTER TEN
Annie's Husband

He is a handsome man with thick, grey hair. He will quickly tell others in the support group that he and Annie have been married for fifty-two years. Annie's husband walks with a cane intended to support a bum knee and years of caregiving stress. He feels very alone in his battle to **do right** by Annie. He struggles daily with how much time to spend with his wife and then, with how much time he has available to do nothing. Annie was the planner. She was the go-getter who always arranged their social life. Now, she barely remembers her name.

Annie's husband has struggled emotionally since placing Annie in the House. He is intensely angry at the maladaptive behaviors Annie exhibits when he visits. He never knows which Annie will be presented to him and he is constantly on guard. Sometimes, Annie is socially gregarious and pleasant to her husband and to those residing in the House. At other times, she spews anger and resentment as easily as a lawn spreader throwing forth fertilizer.

Annie's husband oftentimes spends an inordinate amount of time in Annie's room and no one is sure what occurs in there. Even though the door is open and anyone can enter, it is as if time has frozen in the life of Annie's husband, and, he is simply there.

Even though others in the support group have told Annie's husband he rightfully should be angry at the vicious disease that has robbed him of the gentle times and the joy of the early relationship, he tends to personalize the aberrant the moods of his wife.

Annie's husband cannot help but hate the current behaviors as well. He has no one to support him other than the support group and an hour of support once a month simply is not enough to compensate for the ongoing onslaught of negativity during the visits with the little-known woman he calls his wife.

Some members of the support group are worried about Annie's husband. But then, one day, the worry is replaced by delight as the emotionally-elusive man tells a tale that seems to come right out of the mouth of Mark Twain himself. He tells a delightful story about how he once got an article submitted to the Library of Congress in such detail that he pulls in the group members until the final five words when he says, *And then, I woke up!*

The man is encouraged to write more and to reveal more of himself as other group members have done. But, Annie's husband is finished for the day. Perhaps, he is literally finished trying. Charlie's wife is seriously concerned even though Annie's husband assures everyone that he is coping well and that he will *get through it.*

Will's wife and Charlie's wife both know you don't get *through* this disease. Only the release gets you to the next stage. The staff will sing songs and dispense medicine. Housekeeping will clean up spills of various forms and no one will ever ask the nature of the clean-up contents.

The Activities Director will always have trivia questions and art projects and parties to plan. Anita will sing *You are my Sunshine, my only sunshine* daily as she coaxes Ben back to his chair and Esther will always have a boyfriend to keep her dreams intact. Sometimes, you will see Pat, the facility Director putting drywall patch on the walls as she tries to keep the facility from looking battered and worn, but her efforts are always a step behind the next wheel chair crash.

Those who visit regularly understand there is only one thing that keeps the facility running effectively. It is not excessive government regulations and it is not the effort of those who think *this is just a job until something better comes along.* What glues the facility together and allows it to truly serve the residents is the fact that everyone who works there knows Will's name, and Barbara's name, and Charlie's name, and Esther's name............

***

"The fear of death follows from the fear of life. A man who lives fully is prepared to die at any time."

Mark Twain

CHAPTER ELEVEN
Charlie's Wife

When Charlie's wife gets to the double locked door, she hears Annie yelling at staff, calling them all **idiots**. Beth stands in front of Annie as she punches in the code to open the left door to let in Charlie's wife.

As Charlie's wife enters, she immediately looks at Annie, saying, *Annie, I'm so surprised you're not in the butterfly garden today. It's absolutely gorgeous outside!* Annie replies to the well-intentioned misdirection by commenting, *They're all fuckin' crazy in here and I've had enough.* She turns and leaves to go back down the hallway as Beth simply shrugs at Charlie's wife.

Charlie is nowhere to be found so his wife asks to be let out to the butterfly garden to check on her husband's whereabouts. Charlie is sitting, with his head slumped into his chest, obviously catching a nap in the shaded canopy area. There are butterflies flitting around all the new foliage and is smells like fresh rain outside. Charlie's wife thinks what a shame it is that Charlie has once again missed out on the natural spender of life. But she does not awaken him.

There is a lot of chatter under the canopy today, but most of it is among the three aides who sit diligently by the residents, many of whom are oblivious to the environment. Lettie comes out to dispense medication, careful to administer first to those who are awake. She points to the butterflies and hugs those who reach out to her.

Brianna is laughing at something Anita said and Leonard awakens and shouts out *No you can't. I'm gonna be the one to stop you.* Lettie takes that brief opportunity to put two pills into Leonard's mouth and then she hands him a small cup of thickened water to wash down the pills. Leonard glares at her momentarily and then drops his head to regain visions of his imaginary world. Or, perhaps it is a real world in a parallel universe.

Using her left leg to move her wheelchair, Barbara approaches Charlie's wife and she asks *Is he okay?* Charlie's wife touches Barbara's good arm and she assures the woman that Charlie is just sleeping. Barbara smiles at the touch and she comments *He's a good guy and I wouldn't want him to be dead.* Charlie's wife smiles back and says that yes, Charlie is, indeed, a very good man. For some reason, Barbara's comment has caused Charlie's wife to flash back to a day during a Hawaiian vacation when Charlie presented her with a fresh flower each morning. She always wore the flower in her hair that day. She thinks it is strange how things are triggered in the mind. The involuntary images seem so incongruent with the reality of the present day, and yet, they are sorely welcomed by Charlie's wife.

Charlie stirs and his wife takes the opportunity to cup his chin and raise his head so that his eyes are level with hers. Charlie's eyes open and attempt to focus. And then, he reaches out his left hand to his wife and touches her cheek as if they were young and strong and so much in love. *Hey Buddy,* she says and she understands that Charlie remains with this world. It is a world in which his wife is more and more the stranger, but she will take what is left as that is all that is offered.

Charlie's wife notices that Charlie now reaches almost

exclusively with his left hand as the dominant right hand will no longer voluntarily release itself from the grasp which obliterates any suggestion of fingernails.

Even when his wife rubs his arm and his wrist and his clenched fist, it fails to yield to encouragement. Jackie comes over to explain that they will trim his nails and they will add a cotton roll to Charlie's right palm after applying salve. That will help to prevent infection when the nails attempt to cut the skin of the palm.

Charlie's wife silently mourns the fact that she can no longer cut her husband's nails. For many years, it was an intimate experience for them both. Just last week, she could cut Charlie's nails.

Chuck has just brought Henry outside and he is already screaming. Chuck stops pushing Henry in his chair and he points to the butterflies circling a bed of flowers. Henry stops his tirade and is momentarily mesmerized by the insects. A black and orange butterfly lands on Chuck's shoulder, scaring Henry with its closeness. Henry immediately screams *Oh no, oh no, incoming!*

With grace and agility, Chuck rises and turns Henry's chair so that he is facing the back of the House. *We're going to the air raid shelter, Henry. Just hang on, we're almost there.* And as soon as Chuck opens the door and slides Henry and his chair inside, Henry calms and simply stares at nothing.

Nothing gets past the eyes and ears of Charlie's wife. She watches it all. She studies the comings and goings as if she were the lead researcher on a top-secret project. She stares because she must reassure herself that she can yield Charlie's needs to the care of people better trained and more competent. She is jarred from her own needs back to those of her husband when Charlie says, *Will peed today.* When his wife comments

that we all do that every day, Charlie volunteers, *He did it today, in his pants, in the lunch room.*

And, immediately, Charlie's wife feels horrible. She understands that Will's wife is now undergoing another transition.

It is a transition Will's wife had been dreading, the point at which her husband would become incontinent. Charlie's wife will call Will's wife to see if they can have lunch together. But then, she thinks who is she to think she can comfort someone else's private pain. All she can do is try. She might be the only one that day who will try to comfort Will's wife. That must count for something.

***

"Everybody will die, but very few people want to be reminded of the fact."
Lemony Snicket, The Austere Academy

CHAPTER TWELVE
THE OFFICE VISIT

Charlie has fallen again and this time, he hits his head. He is scheduled to see a neurologist a few days later.

Charlie's wife meets the medical transport van at the doctor's office. Charlie and an aide are already seated. Charlie's face brightens as his wife enters the office. Stacey, the aide had previously accompanied Charlie for a visit to the office of Charlie's treating urologist. While Stacey and Charlie's wife talk, the older woman gets a genuine appreciation for many of the staff at the House. Stacey volunteers that she has worked in her position as an aide for twenty-four years and that **I wouldn't dream of doing anything else.**

When Charlie is called into the office for examination, Stacey remains outside and Charlie's wife wheels her husband into the interview room. Extensive history is taken and Charlie then undergoes some testing. His wife has brought in relevant documents from previous testing along with the results of a previous MRI (Magnetic Resonance Imaging) of Charlie's brain. The MRI was several years old and would be used to compare to current testing results.

After quite some time, the neurologist enters the office. He has the testing materials in his left hand and he seems to already have reviewed the documents. He asks about Charlie's current placement and Charlie's wife volunteers that the placement had been necessitated by a recent hospitalization. Charlie is not volunteering any information, so the doctor finally directs a question to him, motioning for Charlie's wife to remain silent.

"Well Doctor Douglas," says the neurologist. I would like you to tell me where you are now, who you are with and why you are here."

Charlie's wife gulps because it is highly unlikely Charlie can respond to the three-faceted question.

Charlie thinks for a moment and then says, "Well I am here in your office to comply with your wishes and I am here with this lovely woman."

The neurologist smiles and then puts both hands into the air saying, "He must have had incredible brain cell density!" Charlie's wife smiles in agreement.

Charlie is then removed from the office by the doctor's assistant. His wife whispers to the assistant that Charlie will need to find Stacey. Charlie voices no objection to being removed from the office.

The neurologist then asks Charlie's wife what she thinks of her husband diagnostically. Being a Clinical Psychologist, Charlie's wife cannot formally diagnosis her own husband but she relates the symptoms she has observed over the past nearly-eleven years and she gives them diagnostic titles.

Charlie had never been fully and clearly diagnosed as his multidimensional presentation was never present at any one time. The neurologist agrees to all the diagnoses suggested by Charlie's wife and in addition, he adds, "He's having silent seizures, and one of them will be bigger, probably soon." Charlie's wife closes her eyes, simultaneously wanting and rejecting the information.

Charlie and Stacey are waiting in the reception area when Charlie's wife is finished with the consult. The women walk out together, with Charlie's wife pushing her husband's chair. When the medical van arrives, Charlie's wife kisses her husband good-bye and she gets into her car where she sits, unable to leave while processing what she had just heard. Her brave and brilliant husband had coped for over a decade with a half- dozen illnesses, each of which could have taken his life. Now, she hopes that when her time comes, she can rage so valiantly against the dying of the light.

The following day, Stacey would tell Charlie's wife that her conversation with Charlie on the way back to the facility was very lively. Stacey had asked what Charlie did for a living and he had told Stacey he was undercover for the Navy. Stacey then asked if he could tell her about his mission and he had replied, **Surely you must know I cannot talk about a secret mission**!

Charlie's wife marveled that among the sticky plaques and the neuron bundles and tangles in Charlie's brain, her husband had momentarily accessed a bit of his wit and intellect at such an opportune time. At first, she had felt cheated that she hadn't gotten all of Charlie's mental gifts for the rest of her life. But later, she felt grateful that she had been a privileged recipient of that wit for such an important part of her own life.

***

Stacey and Charlie get back to the House as the evening meal is being readied to serve. Stacey wheels Charlie into the dining room commenting that Will is already there waiting for Charlie. **Who's Will?** Charlie asks. Stacey instinctively feels sad for Charlie. But, that thought of compassion is soon replaced by the feeling of privilege that she had been allowed a brief glimpse into the window of Charlie's soul.

***

"Life should not be a journey to the grave with the intention of arriving safely in a pretty and well-preserved body, but rather to skid in broadside in a cloud of smoke, thoroughly use up, totally worn out, and loudly proclaiming, 'Wow, what a ride!'"
Hunter S. Thompson

CHAPTER THIRTEEN
Will's Wife

After entering the secured unit, Will's wife immediately looks to the left. Some residents are playing balloon volleyball, but her husband is not one of the players. Neither is he an onlooker. He is not in the room. She proceeds down the hallway and makes a left turn where she walks down the length of the hallway to the next-to-last room on the right. Will is not in the room. She enters anyway as she has freshly-washed and dried laundry to place in the closet and the bureau drawer.

Atop the bureau is a pair of Depends. Will's wife checks and they are wet. She wraps them in a plastic bag and places the soiled undergarment in the wastepaper basket in the adjacent bathroom. Will's bathroom, like all the bathrooms in the House has only a toilet and a sink. There is a call button for those who need help. There is also a wastepaper basket which usually has a good deal of trash around it.

Most of the residents cannot seem to find the wide top rim of the plastic basket. Will's wife smiles as she remembers Charlie's wife telling her that Charlie has gotten very compulsive the past few months and there is never any trash anywhere in his bathroom. She has no idea what Charlie does with his trash but then, she remembers Charlie's wife telling her about a $250 plumbing job when Charlie stuffed his Depends down the toilet while he was still living at home.

Will's shirts are carefully hung in his closet. His wife looks around the room, trying to decide whether to locate her husband. She is exhausted today and she wouldn't mind skipping a visit. She proceeds out the door and down the hallway, glancing inside rooms as she makes her way.

Will's Wife knows her husband no longer has any comprehension of days or hours, or even minutes. She spots Will sleeping in Harry's room. She enters and looks at her husband who is soundly sleeping. He looks fully invested in the sleep process and she elects not to disturb him.

As she passes the nursing station, Will's wife says to Will's nurse Lettie, *Will is in Harry's room if you need him for meds, Lettie,* and Lettie thanks Will's wife and comments, *Thanks, I'll remember to change the sheets as soon as he's awake.*

Only months ago, it would have horrified Will's wife to think her husband was sleeping in someone else's bed. But now, she realizes that in the grand scheme of things, it is comforting for the residents to know that when they are tired, they have a place to sleep. Furthermore, residents are not chastised for doing something *wrong.* It is nothing more than that.

As she gets to the juncture by the nursing station, she remembers to inquire about Charlie. Chuck has just checked in on him and he says that Charlie is now taking naps in the afternoon. Will's wife asks if Charlie is okay and Chuck comments that *Charlie is slowing down now.* And, Will's wife knows exactly what that means.

As the two are talking, Lettie calls out, *Oh, Clara, you're wearing your birthday suit and it isn't even your birthday!. Lettie* takes Clara's hand and gently steers her down the hallway saying, *Sweetheart, it's a bit chilly today for what you don't have on.*

As she walks Clara back to her room, Lettie thinks how lovely is the name Clara. It is a bit old-fashioned, but it is a strong, no-nonsense name. Lettie tells Clara they are playing a game called *Put Your Hands Here*. **Lettie** places her hands on her own crotch and asks Clara to do the same. She praises Clara when the smallish and vulnerable woman complies. Chuck shrugs and Will's wife smiles as she proceeds down the hallway to be let out of the Memory Care Unit of the House.

As the right side of the double doors is opened, Will's wife hears the concerned voice of a spouse informing staff, *There's someone sleeping in my husband's bed! I want him out of there right now!* Will's wife shakes her head and proceeds out the door. She thinks to herself that the poor woman has not yet figured out that this place is not the story of The Three Bears; it is life in the House. She knows the staff will handle the *issue* with calmness and dignity. She has no hesitation is leaving the House for the day.

***

"When people don't express themselves, they die one piece at a time."
> **Laurie Halse Anderson**

CHAPTER FOURTEEN
Unreported Abuse

There is shouting and screaming in the hallway as Charlie's wife visits with her husband in his room. Sticking her head out the doorway, Charlie's wife sees Lettie running down the hallway calling out, **No, no, Annie. Clara is not trying to kill you. Please Annie.**

Clara has her hands up to her face in a defensive position and she is cowering from the taller-than-average Annie. As soon as Lettie reaches the duo, Annie begins to pound on Lettie. She scratches Lettie's face before Noah can get to the group and pull Lettie away to safety. Then, Clara begins to call out violently, **Someone is killing me; someone is killing me!** Lettie takes Clara protectively in her arms and slowly walks her down the hallway and back to her room. Lettie is angry when she glances at the nursing station and sees the Medical Director glued to his chair, reviewing case notes. Surely, he heard the altercation.

When Clara is calmed, Lettie goes back to check on Annie who has now forgotten about her tirade. Chuck is talking with Annie about her former job and he is doing a great job of refocusing the woman.

Lettie goes back to the nursing station and the Medical Director remains in Lettie's chair so she lets herself into the small family visiting room. It is not long before Jerri enters. Spontaneously, Lettie says, "I just don't know how much longer I can take it."

Jerrie goes to touch her arms and she comments on the facial scratches. "I know," Jerri says. There is no more to be said. Both women know that Lettie and Jerri will be there tomorrow and the next day and the next. It is all just part of the job.

"Bernie got me again," Jerrie says matter-of-factly.
"Oh, crap – the urinal?" Lettie asks.
"Yep, a full load," Jerrie replies. "I think he was saving it up for me."

Both nurses return to the nursing station. Lettie is relieved that the doctor is gone and she doesn't have to try to explain her scratches. Jerrie gets out gauze and antiseptic and gently dabs at the scratches. They are superficial and will heal quickly.

The husband of a new admission comes up to the nursing station complaining that his wife is **Sleeping a lot and that's not good for her.** As Charlie's wife approaches the nursing station, Jerri comes out and heads to the room of the new admission. Jerri's lips are taut with tension but she says nothing. From having information in the resident's chart, she knows fully well that the woman has been sleeping most of the day for several months now while in her husband's care at home. She further understands that complaining to the staff is simply a means for the man to let off steam at his own sense of inadequacy. Or, perhaps, this is his way of assuring himself that he is monitoring his wife's condition.

Sometimes, abuse occurs but it is not a reportable incident. It will be noted in the patient's chart and sometimes, there is a medication adjustment following a case review. But the incident will not be reported to the State even though several people have been abused on this single day in the house of final release.

***

"It is a curious thing, the death of a loved one. We all know that our time in this world is limited, and that eventually all of us will end up underneath some sheet, never to wake up. And yet, it is always a surprise when it happens to someone we know. It is like walking up the stairs to your bedroom in the dark, and thinking there is one more stair than there is. Your foot falls down, through the air, and there is a sickly moment of dark surprise as you try and readjust the way you thought of things."

Lemony Snicket, Horeradish

CHAPTER FIFTEEN
Annie's Husband

Annie's husband continues to vacillate about how he should think about his wife. He knows she has a diseased brain. But, she uses no aides to walk and her vocabulary continues to astound most of those who care for her. He wants to think that Annie's disease will *pass* and she will come back to him. But, he is a very intelligent man and he knows better than to even consider that a possibility.

He won't go to dinner after the support group has adjourned. He feels out of synch with the female members. Annie's husband believes he thinks differently because he is a man but in truth, he thinks differently because he has not yet truthfully conceptualized what is happening in his life. He is like Goldilocks who keeps trying out new beds in hopes that one of them will fit *just right*. And, in truth, Annie's husband cannot even fathom running out of beds to try.

Annie and her husband sit in the dining room at a round table. She looks about the room, trying to find some means to interpret her surroundings. Her husband looks around as well, hoping he might find direction that will help him to accept the nightmare into which he has involuntarily become a player. He talks with those who bother to stop and talk with him. Charlie's wife has come over and she directs her comments both to Annie and to her husband. Annie's husband listens to the ease with which Charlie's wife relates to his wife and he studies the interactions. He could easily talk with his wife as well. And, he will do just that – as soon as he finds her again.

A plane goes over and it triggers something in Henry. This time, he is not easily comforted. Two aides are with him and it is not enough. He begins to thrash around and the aides fear Henry will hurt himself. Beth runs out of the room while James continues to hold Henry's hands so he will not injure his face. When the demons come, Henry reaches for his face and pulls at his cheeks as if to pull out all the bad memories.

Jerri comes in with a mobile tray filled with medications which are about to be administered before dinner. She calls out Henry's name and she tells him *Everyone is safe, Henry. You are safe and your family is with you. No one is hurt, Henry.* And she calms him with an injection. James continues to hold Henry as his limbs become numb and he exhales as if he has simply returned to the living world. Beth and James continue to talk and soon, Henry is himself. At least, he is the part of himself that is not caught in the ongoing nightmare of his years of service in Viet Nam.

Henry's picture is up on the Wall of Heroes in the entryway. Charlie's picture is hung beside those of Will and Louie. There are over three dozen military men currently in the House and most of them understand Henry's need to rid himself of his demons. They watch the incident and they appear pleased that Henry has been treated with respect.

Charlie's wife smiles at Jerri. She silently concludes that no one could realistically challenge the woman's competence. In fact, no one tends to challenge Jerri at all. There is a look about Jerrie that cautions others to keep their distance so that she can go about her business unimpeded.

But, Charlie's wife also likes the aire of compassion which seems to go so easily with the medical skills. Jerri only shows that vulnerability during private times with her most vulnerable patients. She has done this for over two decades now and there is not much she has not seen or experienced first-hand. Charlie's wife comments to Annie's husband on Jerri's demeanor but Annie's husband simply shrugs and says *What a waste.* Not knowing to whom the comment is directed, Charlie's wife simply remains silent.

Silently, Charlie's wife disagrees that any of the lives have been in vain. Her mind reassures itself that these lives are not being wasted at all. Rather, they are being honored and respected while the souls are awaiting the moment of release.

***

"Often you shall think your road impassable, somber and companionless. Have will and plod along, and round each curve you shall find a new companion."
Mikhail Naimy, The Book of Mirdad

CHAPTER SIXTEEN
Will's Wife

She doesn't want to go to the House today: she is weary, again. Even now when the caregiving duties are shared, she cannot seem to experience a feeling of rest in her body and in her mind. But she goes anyway, for that is what Will's wife does. That is what they all do.

Will's wife walks down the hallway toward her husband's room. Staff has told her Will continues to refuse showering by the staff, so his wife goes to clean him. The thought of having him unclean is not yet an image she is ready to accept or even tolerate.

Will is standing with his back facing his wife as she enters the room. His diapers are sagging and he struggles to pull them down so that they can rest on his pants. His wife comes up behind him and says, **Here, let me help you** and Will simply stands, hanging onto his walker. **We're going to the shower,** she says. She pulls up the diaper and pulls up Will's pants and they head to the shower room. Will does not protest.

Just down the hall is a large shower room. Residents are not allowed to have showers in their rooms in the memory care unit. It is a safety issue and, like all issues in the House, it is regulated by the State.

Not too many years ago, an aide left a higher--functioning resident in the shower alone, at the request of the resident. The resident then had a heart attack, dropping to the tile floor. She was found a minute later. The aide had been right outside the door, respecting the rights to privacy of the woman inside. There is little the aide could have done but nevertheless, regulations now prohibited those in memory care from showering alone. And, of course, the House was put on probation.

The showering room is huge. It is fully tiled in a light tan tile, with variations of the color on the non-slip tiled floor. The room contains two separate showers. Both are equipped with curtains and flexible showerheads that detach so the resident can be sprayed clean by attendants without getting wet themselves. A shower aide can move fully around the resident, showering, scrubbing and shampooing while the resident either stands or sits on a safety bench. Some residents require a lift to get to shower seating from a wheelchair and that is available as well. Those resident unable to get to the shower room are given sponge baths in their beds.

Across from the showers are a sink, a toilet and a large vanity with a mirror. They are partitioned by curtains for resident privacy. There is a large cart in the center of the room. It contains soaps, shampoos, tooth brushes and tooth paste. There are also hair dryers, lotions and deodorants. For the resident, there is a spa-like feeling in the shower room. Even those who initially resist the showering routine generally end up pacified after being pampered in the shower room. Will is one of those residents. At some point in time, he will give the showering routine authority to staff but, for now, having his wife shower him is a way for him to control just a tiny portion of his life.

Male and female residents are not allowed in the shower room at the same time. So, on some days, Will's wife must wait until a female resident is showered, groomed and dressed before she can take Will in for his shower. But, today, they are lucky. No one is in the shower room.

Will's wife takes him into the far shower and she helps Will to remove his clothes. She tosses the wet diaper into the trash can where housekeeping will soon remove it. The dirty clothes will be folded and taken home to wash. When Will is undressed, the shower is turned on and adjusted to temperature. Sometimes, Will helps to rub the soap on his body and at other times, he is content to have his wife scrub his body. On occasion, they both have images of times long ago when they pleasured one another in the shower. But, it is difficult for Will's wife to allow those images she can no longer experience. As for Will, he has no idea that it has been years since he last pleasured his wife.

After his body is cleaned, Will's wife shampoos her husband's hair and gives him a full rinse with the detachable shower head. He is in seventh heaven with the attention. She flashes back to when she used to bathe her own children and she smiles.

Will receives help from his wife to towel dry and dress. He is already shaved so she does not need to do that chore today. She seats Will at the vanity and blow dries his hair, taking care to style it just right after the very short haircut he has gotten three days before. He is content and she is satisfied. She feels it was the right thing to do, to come to the House today.

There is entertainment at the House again and, with the door open, the musical strains drift down the hall. When Will and his wife leave the shower room, she hears a female performer singing the song "Crazy."

The song seizes Will's wife almost to the point of having stomach cramps and she feels queasy. She's just not prepared to hear those lyrics today. But, nevertheless, the performer belts out the words to Patsy Cline's "Crazy":

Crazy, I'm crazy for feeling so lonely
Crazy, for feeling so blue
I knew you'd love me as long as you wanted
And then some day
You'd leave me for somebody new.
Worry, why do I let myself worry?
Wondering what in the world did I do?

Will's wife wonders if she can stand long enough to get Will to the dining room where the entertainment is currently keeping the attention of most of the residents. She spots David at a table with only one other occupant and she rushes her husband to a seat near David. She kisses him and tells him she will be back. She knows she will not be back today, but Will has no comprehension

Crazy for thinking that my love could hold you
I'm crazy for trying
And crazy for crying
And I'm crazy for loving you.

She must go to Will's room to pick up the rest of her laundry. As she passes the nursing station, a woman she has not seen before is sitting in a wheelchair, crying and looking lost. She wants to comfort the woman but she feels lost herself and she is fresh out of compassion and giving. An aide comes to the woman as Will's wife hurries on. She races to Will's room and gathers up the clothes in the hamper, placing everything in a large plastic bag.

When she approaches the nursing station, there is the

new woman, still in the wheel chair. She is no longer crying. Silent and sullen Frank is sitting beside her in his own chair. He is holding her hand. Both are sharing a moment that neither understands contextually and yet, they both understand pain and they both understand comfort. Will's wife is emotionally captured by the moment but then, she heads for the marred, double white steel doors, hoping that someone will punch in the code in record time so that she can breathe again.

As she gets within ten feet of the door to the world outside, Esther comes down the hallway, screaming that someone has attacked her in her room. *Look at me, I'm all bloody*, she yells as she looks accusingly at Annie who is simply walking in to see the entertainment. An aide comes to access the code to let Will's wife out. Will is sitting, apparently engaged in conversation with David. As Will's wife races through the doors, Annie gives a look of astonishment to Esther who has not a mark on her and she says *Crazy, the whole bloody lot of them*.

As she steps out the front door onto the small, exterior foyer, Will's wife gasps for air. She thinks she might be safe from her own emotional fragility when Bert's wife approaches her. Will's wife wants nothing other than get into her car, get home and have a glass of wine. But she listens while Bert's wife explains that Leonard's wife is failing badly.

Leonard's wife is in the support group and Will's wife very much wants Leonard's wife to be okay. She digs her fingernails into the palms of her hands as she visualizes the group members giving up, one by one. She cannot allow that. She is one of the group herself. Will's wife visualizes her support group as a collection of upright dominoes. If one falls, the others all go as well.

***

"God surely did not create us, and cause us to live, with the sole end of wishing always to die. I believe in my heart, we were intended to prize life and enjoy it, so long as we retain it. Experience never was originally meant to be that useless, blank, pale, slow-trailing thing it often becomes to many, and is becoming to me, among the rest."
Charlotte Bronte

CHAPTER SEVENTEEN
Charlie's Wife

She's getting scared now. Charlie has been in the House for twelve weeks and he is getting worse. At first, he was worse by the week and now, he seems worse by the day. When first admitted, he could get up from his wheelchair and walk. And then, he could get up and use the walker. But now, Charlie stays in the chair and he needs assistance just to stand. Charlie's wife knows in the intelligent regions of her mind that this decline is inevitable but, her heart wants to run to a place of comfort and safety, to the years long ago.

In the dining room, Esther waves to Charlie's wife in a greeting that cannot be ignored. She goes to Esther's table and is surprised that Charlie is the one with his back to her. She thinks he might be shrinking, shrinking from life in general. Esther is stroking Charlie's right arm as the tremors persist. Wasn't it just two days ago that Esther stoked Charlie's arm and it soothed him and stopped the tremors? Charlie's wife is both awed and horror-struck at the same time. Can people be standing and functional one week and nearly paralyzed and mute the next?

No one seems to have any answers concerning Charlie's diseases. Everyone is matter-of-fact about treating the symptoms and not terribly worried that the symptoms are in flux. Jerri acknowledges that **Charlie if failing.**

Charlie's wife knows that her husband's diseases are now in charge and she is but a bystander. She hates the feelings of loss of control. For so many years, she had kept Charlie going. She had comforted him and made him feel safe. She now searches her mind for images of even tiny ways she can comfort her husband and she is drawing nothing but blanks.

Esther is talking nonstop about another elaborate delusion. On this occasion, she is the physician's wife and she is busy getting shots ready for those being treated by her husband. Esther points to two staff members and says, *See how they respond so quickly to my instructions.* Charlie's wife looks to where Esther points and she sees Will's nurse Letti coming in to the dining room, wheeling the medications cart. She must smile despite her grief. She silently thinks how beautifully everything and everyone in the House fit so perfectly into Esther's delusions.

The food carts have also appeared and there is a general restlessness while everyone awaits their specially-prepared trays. After reading the resident's name on a piece attached to a tray, the attendant brings the tray to the correct table and places it before the resident, removing the cover and making a personal comment such as *Looks like your lucky day today, Bob.*

Some eagerly attack the food placed in front of them and others make comments and shove the food inches from where it was placed. They wait for an attendant or an aide to come by and give them personal attention by prodding them to eat. In the meantime, they make comments such as *Pure slop,* or *You have a lot of nerve feeding this garbage to me. Think I'm a pig or something?*

Not long ago, Charlie would have ravaged everything on his plate before the last resident was served. Now, he struggles to pick up his fork with his left hand. His right hand is in such a tight fist that a trickle of blood runs down the base of his fist and onto the blue tablecloth.

The wad of cotton put in Charlie's fist falls from his hand. Charlie's wife picks up the cotton and dabs at the blood while Charlie struggles with the fork. He has managed to stab a green bean and bring it to his mouth. But, that single, prolonged act will be his only self-feeding success for the day.

Anna and Clara come in late. They are both in clean dresses, with Clara holding a small bag with a chain over her shoulder. They are holding hands and they sit together at a table talking as if they have recently gone on a shopping spree and now require a break. The food attendant notices them and immediately brings their trays. An observer might think the two women have preordered room service and it has just been delivered.

While Anna and Clara chat over roast turkey with gravy and mashed potatoes and green beans, Millie comes over in her wheel chair. She has unbuttoned her blouse and she exposes her bare chest to Charlie's wife. Bonnie spots the social infraction and she sprints to the table, closing Millie's blouse and redirecting the woman to her table. Millie swats at Bonnie as the aide tries to rebutton Millie's blouse but Bonnie is undaunted. She begins to distract Millie with a tale about Thanksgiving dinner in the time of the pilgrims and Millie takes a bite of her mashed potatoes. *Shame on you!* Millie shouts to Bonnie as she chews on her turkey.

Esther has observed the incident between Millie and Bonnie. *She's very disturbed*, Esther explains to Charlie's wife. Esther periodically reaches over trying to pry open Charlie's right hand. She is clearly puzzled that her once-healing touch no longer appears effective. *He needs physical therapy*, she says. Charlie's wife replies that she will keep that in mind.

As Charlie's wife continues to feed her husband, Bonnie returns to the table and takes Charlie's right hand in hers, trying to encourage him to open his right hand.

Bonnie gradually gets the fist opened enough to swab the fingernail wounds with water and a fresh napkin while she apologizes to Charlie's wife for not trimming the nails closer to the quick. Charlie is invested in chewing a small piece of roasted turkey fed to him by his wife. He appears oblivious to those servicing him.

Bonnie explains how they generally have a roll of gauze in Charlie's hand to prevent him from digging into his palm. As if reading her mind, Bonnie says *They don't seem to have any control over those hand spasms. I won't forget again.* Charlie's wife smiles her appreciation for Bonnie's care and she gets a generous forkful of mashed potatoes for Charlie. She is almost afraid to feed him meat unless it is ground. Even with the thickened water, Charlie sometimes chokes on his food and he gets afraid to eat more. Or, perhaps, he is simply not hungry these days. She remembers how before Charlie entered the House, she frequently had to do the Heimlich. She marvels at how she took such drastic action as common place.

Charlie's wife notices that Will is sitting at the table next to them. He has again pushed away his lunch tray and concentrated on the pudding. Lettie tries to encourage him to eat the entree while giving him his one o'clock medications. She shrugs and leaves the table to dispense medications to others, returning a short while later with a bottle of Ensure.

Will takes the carton and drinks eagerly. Lettie has told him it is a chocolate shake in a bottle.

Once Will has finished his Ensure, Charlie's wife turns and asks what is happening with him. Charlie turns his head as well and it surprises his wife that he wants to follow the conversation. *I'm going home today*, Will declares.

Even though Charlie's wife knows that event will not occur, she remarks that it's nice that Will can look forward to things like that. Then, abruptly, Will gets up, takes his walker and says *I have a delivery to make.* He leaves the dining room and enters the hallway. Charlie's wife wonders which room Will is going to nap in today as he can only rarely find his own room. She hopes it is a room that will help him to sleep and forget deliveries he is no longer capable of making.

Charlie has finished his mashed potatoes, with just slight amounts of turkey and a green bean or two. He slumps slightly in his chair and refuses more food. He is not responsive to his wife for about fifteen seconds. Then, he looks at her and he smiles. She knows he has had another silent seizure. She kisses Charlie and then, she goes to tell Jerri about the recent episode. Jerri says *I know* and both women understand that the seizures and the transient ischemic attacks are becoming more and more frequent and that the **Big One** is only a matter of time.

She doesn't feel like visiting others today and Jerri has already said she will get Charlie and put him down for a nap. Charlie's wife is so very grateful for those who can offer kindness and respect to her husband when she is simply too tired to function in that role on this day. Charlie is one of those people for whom releasing from life is very hard work. And, on this day, Charlie's wife wants to leave with feelings of respect and admiration for her man. She does not want to take away feelings of hopelessness and helplessness and so, she is content for Jerri to put her husband to bed.

***

"So comes snow after fire, and even dragons have their endings."
J.R.R Tolkien, The Hobbit

CHAPTER EIGHTEEN
The Not-S0-Young and the Restless

It is the weekend at the House and the not-so-young are restless. Sally is eighty-five years old and her once-flexible back is now flexible for another reason. She used to be a trapeze artist with the Ringling Circus but years of arthritic growth and years of living have left her with a spine that betrays her. She is sitting in the dining room and has slipped from her wheelchair. She has a tray across the arms of the chair to discourage her being dislodged but Sally has managed to shift her weight and slump down into the chair. Her head rests against the bottom of the backrest. The tray has secured Sally under her arms, preventing her total escape from the chair.

Residents coming into the dining room will notice Sally's predicament but, as Sally does not seem particularly concerned, they remain unconcerned as well. Then, Anita notices Sally's entrapment and she runs to help her saying, *Oh my gosh, Sally, you've really done a good trick there!*

Anita instructs Jackie to get a support pillow while she works at the tray release to free Sally from her acrobat-like position in the wheel chair. When Jackie returns, Anita places the pillow between Sally's shoulders and the chair back to try to bring a measure of comfort to Sally while she continues to work on the stubborn tray release. Sally's arms are securely pushing on the tray so that the release will not give. Jackie attempts to raise Sally in the chair but Sally's once-limber body is now dead weight which will not be encouraged to budge.

Annie enters the dining room, looks about and she goes to Sally's chair. She looks over the situation and says, *If you sit like that much longer, you will wreck your back.* Jackie escorts Annie to her table and tells her to sit as it is snack time. Annie continues to look at the wheel chair-trapped resident with a great deal of interest but she offers no further advice.

As Beth begins to serve the snacks, Ben immediately goes over to the first-served resident and grabs a cookie, stuffing it in his mouth before anyone can deter him from his daily mission. One way or another, Ben is determined to be served first. As a corporate executive, he was always served first in the boardroom.

Anita has seen Ben's theft and she asks Jackie to attend to Sally's safety while she skillfully turns Ben around and redirects him to his table singing, *You are my sunshine, my only sunshine.* Beth is on top of the situation and she has already put a cookie and a juice at Ben's place setting. No one complains that Ben will get two cookies today. Most residents are relieved that Ben will stay seated for a while and their own treats are now safe for them to enjoy.

In the House, the weekend staff is not necessarily the *regular* staff but that does not mean there is any loss of effectiveness in servicing the needs of the residents.

Louie, Will and Charlie are sitting together at one table. Will has placed his walker in a position so that no one else can get to the fourth chair at the round table. He knows there are many ways to get your way in the House.

Charlie offers that he has recently been to Italy and that the other fellows should think about going there. Will reminds Charlie that he is simply too busy at work to get away now. So, Charlie then remarks that Louie should think about going to Italy and Louie replies that he just might do that. In truth, none of the men has been anywhere for quite some time. The last to go anywhere was Charlie and he went to brunch with his wife thirteen weeks ago, just before he entered the hospital. Charlie thinks he is still in the hospital and he tells his friends he will go back to Italy as soon as the doctor clears him for release. Despite the progression of Charlie's dementia and his delusional thought processing, he remains a well-spoken man and most of the staff can see both the professor and the lieutenant in his demeanor and his verbalizations. They also attend to the authority in Will's voice and the gentleness in Louie's interactions with others. And, the weekend staff also knows everyone by name.

As Anita continues to struggle to release Sally from her awkward wheel chair position, Esther, the lady in the red sweater and Barbara talk at the table next to the all-male table. Barbara is very sad because her potential husband Frank has died. He was carried away in an ambulance and when Barbara asks if he will come back, Lettie gently tells her, *No sweetheart, he won't be coming back here.* Barbara's tears are real.

The lady in the red sweater gets up from her chair and goes to Barbara to comfort her. Barbara has now had this delusion of Frank being her intended for the past two weeks and she is rehearsing it again. It matters not what the delusion is, the pain is real and the understanding of that pain somehow also remains real and true, right until the final breaths of life.

Esther is not content to allow Barbara to garner all the attention at the table, or perhaps, she simply is not into Barbara's delusion on this day. She attempts to distract the lady in the red sweater by volunteering, *Well, my ex-husband is right over there and he's really an ass!*

When no one responds to Esther's declaration, she seems to ponder what other delusion might allow the women at her table to become invested in her. When Beth serves Esther her juice and cookies, Esther perseverates on her initial delusion and she repeats her words out loud to the aide Beth. Beth smiles and simply says, *Oh, Esther, I thought he died a while back.* The statement initially confuses Esther but then she recovers saying, *Well, that's his ghost haunting me then!*

Anita and Jackie yell, *Yah!* Two visitors turn to notice that Sally has been released and is now sitting upright in her chair. At the men's table, Will, Charlie and Louie appear oblivious to the entire situation. At the women's table, Esther babbles on about how her ex-husband is now haunting her. Barbara has quit crying. She seems to have forgotten about Frank's death and she is intent on searching the dining room for the ghost of Esther's ex-husband.

Jean wanders over to the table and sits with the other three women. Esther has apparently had enough attention for snack time on this day and she tells the others that Jean has a beautiful voice. Jean smiles and she begins to sing, *I'll be loving you, always.*

Even though many of the residents of the House are restless, they have developed a marvelous way of remaining young. Many cannot stand; many cannot walk; many cannot toilet themselves and some are unable to feed themselves.

And yet, they are the young and the restless on this weekend in which the weekend staff helps them to feel respected, safe and valued in the house of the final release. Two residents have released that week, but others have come to take their places. The composition remains stable in the House, with issues common to the released also being common to the newly-placed.

***

"The heaviness in her heart hadn't eased, but there was room there for humour too"
Nalo Hopkinson, Brown Girl in the Ring

CHAPTER NINETEEN
Annie's Husband

Annie's husband has been dreading coming to the House and yet, he comes almost driven to come daily. He is frustrated and angry and he doesn't want to live out the rest of his life this way. It is illogical and irrational and totally antithetical to his life pattern of order and discipline. He understands that his feelings could eat away at him, harming his physical being and leaving Annie to live out the rest of her life without him.

He stays in Annie's room a lot, just like Ben's wife stays in the room of her husband. Annie's husband thinks it may now be time to know about the House in which he has placed his wife. So, he begins to look, and he listens to the verbal machinations.

As he is sitting at the dining table with his wife, Annie's husband tunes in to the conversation at the adjacent table. There are two women and two men at the table. One woman appears to be speaking incoherently. She is obviously delusional but the other woman has her full attention.

After a short period, the second woman enters the monologue and the first woman becomes the conversation recipient. The women appear to be adhering to social boundaries. When one speaks the other listens. When there is a reply, the recipient then becomes the conversational leader while the other listens attentively to the apparent gibberish. Annie's husband has no conclusion other than that the women have their own sense of social propriety.

Annie's husband looks at his wife and he wonders if she engages in such conversation. He has been so busy trying to look for any signs of *normal* conformity that he has missed the clever ways in which his wife has adapted to the machinations in her compromised brain. He entertains the notion that perhaps, life remains meaningful to his wife, although in an entirely different way than she had been accustomed prior to the onset of her disease.

He thinks silently that the residents in the House almost seem to be in a parallel universe in which people look the same but they think and act differently based upon the warped information available to them individually and collectively. But still, wouldn't that be the definition of insanity, he wonders. After all, it comes from brains damaged by disease and ravaged by time.

And now, Annie's husband struggles with a different issue altogether. If Annie has a meaningful life, just how can he fit into that life? Even more, should he even try to fit into a world in which thoughts, emotions and behaviors appear aberrant and illogical? He begins to wonder if he is the one who has it all wrong. Maybe he shouldn't visit as much, as he leaves depressed after each visit. His logical brain speculates that, perhaps, the House has its own special set of values and expectations and he is the intruder. He is the one who must learn a different way of knowing and not them. He is the one out of synch in the house of final release.

Now that he has that information, he is hard-pressed to know what to do with it. Annie's husband thinks he will surely compromise his own sense of values acquired from a lifetime of living and experiencing if he accepts the functioning of the House as its own reality. He does not want to let go of his wife and yet, he does not want to let go of himself.

     The two men at the adjacent table have remained silent. But, when Charlie's wife enters the dining room, she immediately pulls up a chair and sits beside her husband and Louie. She asks what is happening on that day. Charlie says, *Not a whole heck of a lot* and Louie shakes his head and says, *That's right.*

     Annie's husband takes note of the fact that Charlie's wife has encouraged the men to tell her about their environment instead of reporting on her own. Unsatisfied with Charlie's noncommittal response, his wife then suggests that it will soon be Easter and she wonders how they should all celebrate.

     Louie lights up and begins to tell about an Easter egg hunt when he was a child. He tells an elaborate story about looking for hours for treats and Charlie is mesmerized. Charlie then volunteers that he never had egg hunts but always thought it would be fun. Charlie's wife ignores the falsity of the memory while Louie explains how eggs are boiled and dyed and decorated and Charlie thinks the eggs must be works of art.

     Both men enter a discussion about what colors they would use. Then Charlie's wife asks them where they would hide the eggs. Charlie becomes excited and he points to places all around the dining room where eggs might be placed. He loves his own suggestion of hiding an egg in the fish tank! Louie suggests a couple of hiding places that Charlie has overlooked like *Right under your ass!* The discussion is a fair competition of like-endowed minds.

As he listens, Annie's husband begins to understand just how memories are worked into present reality and he concludes that there is, indeed, a reality at the House. As the men are talking, Charlie's wife approaches Annie's husband.

Annie has risen from her chair and gone wandering and her husband is not up to wandering with her. Annie's husband smiles at Charlie's wife. He wants to know how she can stimulate the silent men to talk and to have a meaningful social experience on that day. Charlie's wife says she always lets her husband define the parameters of the visit as this is his House and these are his rules. She has given up expecting him to live within social convention as his brain no longer allows that.

But it allows something? Annie's husband asks. *Sure,* Charlie's wife explains, but *different things on different days. I just find out what the brain has offered up to Charlie on any day and then, I just jump on in.* Annie's husband must think about that for several seconds. He thinks it might be disrespectful to encourage delusional thinking and Charlie's wife says kindly but bluntly, *But, isn't it disrespectful not to? After all, that's where he is now.* Another silence follows until Annie's husband says, *But, it's not real. You are encouraging him to stay where reality isn't.*

She smiles. Charlie's wife has heard this from others, others who insist that their loved ones act out the scripts of life they have learned. Finally, she says, *You know, it's going to progress no matter what we do. THEY have to progress with the disease and quite frankly, I want to stay with my Charlie. That means I have to go where he is. Afterwards, I can laugh and I can cry and face my own reality.*

The words seem foreign to the thoughts and emotions tossed around in the mind of Annie's husband. What he brings out of this is, *You mean you laugh at him when you're not here!*

Charlie's wife takes a deep breath of air before she says, *I never laugh at Charlie. But I must laugh at the situation we are both in because it is truly insane. It is so averse to the reality you and I live outside of here. But, Charlie is HERE now, and so is Annie. Why on earth would they want to be reminded via reality of the fact they are dying?*

She smiles at Annie's husband as he bites his lower lip. His eyes glass over and take on a shine. Charlie's wife thinks Annie's husband is an intelligent, dignified and rational man who is in deep do-do emotionally.

***

"The difference between the man who just cuts lawns and a real gardener is in the touching, he said. The lawn cutter might just as well not have been there at all; the gardener will be there a lifetime."
Ray Bradbury, Fahrenheit 451

CHAPTER TWENTY
Will's Wife

She has come to shower her husband today. Will's wife is not happy with the condition of the showers. There is a reddish liquid spattered around the vanity area, with towels on the floor and a general look of disarray. She will bring it to the attention of the staff after she cleans and grooms Will.

When Will is safely seated in the dining room looking alert and freshly scrubbed, His wife mentions to Will's nurse Lettie that the showers need a good scrubbing. She mentions the red liquid, stressing **I hope it is not blood**.

Lettie smiles and assures Will's wife that the shower room will shortly be attended to and that they had *Nonstop customer business all morning* in the shower room. Lettie tells Will's wife that Sharon had asked to have her hair dyed but she had no money in her account for such services.

That casual information stops Will's wife in her mental tracks as she thinks about the implications. *You mean a staff member dyes her hair in the shower room?* she asks. Lettie responds that they have many residents on Medicaid who have no personal funds. The staff does not want them to feel inferior because they cannot afford personal grooming services so staff members routinely do things such as hair and nail services.

It is time for Will's wife to feel a bit sheepish, and she does. She routinely puts money into Will's account so that he can have haircuts and other things normally taken for granted.

But now, she understands that many in the House do not have such luxuries. She thinks about staff members who spend their own earnings on small things for the residents, small things like hair coloring and nail polish. And she thinks about an overworked aide taking the time to color and style a resident's hair and she wants to cry at the small acts of kindness. But, she doesn't.

Instead, Will's wife goes to the shower room, intending to try to help clean up the mess there. But, she is tardy in her good intentions. Maria is already there with her bucket and her mop and she is removing the red from the walls and the floor. And, Maria is stocking new soaps and towels and straitening up the supplies tray. Will's wife remains silent, but she is deeply touched.

***

On this day, Will is to go for an appointment to the local Veterans Administration to have his yearly exam which will keep him eligible for veterans services. Stacey accompanies Will to the appointment in the medical van and Will's wife is to meet them at the VA facility.

Everything goes as scheduled and Will's wife checks in for the appointment. As they are waiting, Will tells the secretary he is hungry and would like something to eat. The secretary finds a bag of chips and gives them to Will. He eagerly attacks the bag of treats and comments on their excellent taste. Will and his wife are then called and escorted into the physician's office. A nurse comes to take *vitals* and to ask a few questions. Will is calm and responsive. He appears to be enjoying the outing. Will's wife is proud of her husband's accommodation to the new setting.

Stacey remains outside in the waiting room. She is

there simply to escort Will to and from the facility, assuring he will be safe and properly attended to. When a family member is available, that member will accompany the resident. Most of the residents of the House are unable to provide a factual history or current status to healthcare professionals. If no family member is available, then Stacey will try her best to provide necessary information.

When the physician comes into the office, Will remains quiet until the physician begins to make demands. *What is the date? Where are you now? Why are you here? Where do you live? How old are you?* **Fold this paper in half. When I drop the paper, I want you to pick it up.** But, these are questions to which answers are no longer available in Will's brain and Will becomes agitated. The physician does not seem to understand how he has unsettled the patient. He continues his questioning and demands, and Will begins to lose control. Will begins to swear at the doctor and he asks his wife to take him home. He begins to act out behaviorally but he is limited in his ability to physically express his anger and frustration because of his confinement to the walker and his general lack of mobility.

Once Will is *set off,* it is difficult to bring any sense of order to the chaos. Will's wife attempts to intervene but he curses at her while demanding to be taken out of the office. The physician is helpless to assuage the chaos he has initiated and he asks Will's wife to remove her husband. All the way down the hallway, Will is cursing. When they get to the waiting room, Stacey stands up in astonishment at the change in Will's demeanor. She immediately calls for transport back to the facility and is told there will be a half an hour wait.

Will's wife is scared but she understands that stability will only occur when Will is again allowed to dwell in the known, and the known is now the House. She asks if she can transport Stacey and Will back to the residential facility in her car and she is given permission to do so.

In the parking lot, Will's wife immediately opens the back door, not giving Will an opportunity to sit up front and influence her driving. Stacey sits by Will so that she can attempt to soothe him. And she does. It takes several minutes of talk about what they will eat and what they will do when they get back. The conversation about the known is soothing for Will and by the time they arrive at the House, Will eagerly uses his walker to traverse the front sidewalk and get into the building. His wife leaves while Stacey escorts Will to the dining room where the world is once again knowable.

Will's wife heaves a huge sigh of relief. The natural heat and humidity of the mid-summer day has only been enhanced and intensified by the outing until Will's wife feels she might choke with emotion and fear. *Has everything been undone?* She asks herself. But no, she stops to comprehend what has just occurred. And then, she is ever-so-proud of her husband. He asked to go back to safety; he asked to go back to the known world. He asked to go home. And, he willingly went in the House with a caring person he trusted. Will's wife thought, *What a wonderful and brave man he has become.* And she took herself home to a full glass of chardonnay.

***

"Were it possible to see further than our knowledge reaches, and yet a little bit beyond the outworks of our divinings, perhaps we would endure our sadness with greater confidence than our joys. For they are the moments when something new has entered into us something unknown; our feelings grow mute in shy perplexity, everything in us withdraws, a stillness comes, and the new, which no one knows, stands in the midst of it, and is silent."
Rainer Maria Rilke, Letters to a Young Poet

CHAPTER TWENTY-ONE
Bonnie and Clive

It is their first visit to the House and they are both stiff and apprehensive. Clive is dressed in a navy-blue business suit with a white shirt and a blue and gold striped tie. It is a hot and sultry Florida day. Clive's greying hair and finely-featured face give the impression of someone pampered and important. His demeanor suggests a middle-aged man who is accostumed to taking control and giving orders. Clive towers over his barely five-foot wife Bonnie who appears to be holding in the potential projectile of the contents of her stomach. She is dressed as if she might be meeting her friends at the country club. Her paisley dress is fashionable and her jewelry is well-matched. Bonnie has a pleasant face that is unable to conceal even a moderate state of anxiety. Neither Clive nor Bonnie has any notion what to expect as they approach the House. Bonnie says, *The flowers are pretty out here, aren't they, Clive?* As usual, Clive responds, *Hmmm*, and the couple proceeds up the sidewalk.

As Clive enters the door to the House, he escorts his wife in and goes directly to the receptionist. Brianna gives a perfunctory greeting and asks how she might help. Clive explains that his mother was *transported* late last evening and he needs to speak with someone in charge. Brianna, who has an uncanny way of knowing who is available at any given moment, calls the Activity Director Tess who appears at the front desk within thirty seconds of the call. Tess takes the couple to introduce them to the Admissions Director who says they should *check in with her* following a visit with Maude.

Bonnie's eyes scan every detail of the area. Clive stares straight ahead, his face a mask of concealed emotions. When the threesome approach the double doors to the memory care unit, Bonnie frowns in disapproval at the chipped paint and the marks on the door. Sharma has punched in the code and she opens the door for the visitors. Immediately, she shouts out, *No, Grandma, you need help there. Just a minute now; we don't want a fall today.* Sharma disappears to assist a resident before Bonnie can offer the simplest greeting.

Tess looks left to the dining area and spots Clive's mother. She is seated at a table with five others, both men and women. They are batting around an inflated balloon. Clive's mother hits the red balloon with her left hand and she appears to be pleased with her success. *It's balloon volleyball,* Tess says to the new visitors. *It's a lot lighter for the residents and they tend to have much more success when they play.* While Bonnie silently processes that it is nice her mother-in-law is already active, Clive says under his breath, *And, I'm paying for this!*

Clive's mother Maude was transported from the hospital the previous evening. She was released to memory care and rehabilitation following six days in the hospital. A left-brain stroke had significantly weakened the right side of her body, necessitating the use of a wheel chair. Maude could not speak and she did not always appear to comprehend attempts to communicate with her. She was however, awake and seemingly alert.

Maude had experienced a stroke five years before the current incident. She experienced an irregular heartbeat and she had become frightened and nearly agoraphobic in her home in England. Clive's sister looked in on her mother for five years and then decided it was time her brother pitched in and did his duty. Clive and his wife decided it was best to bring Mum to the States where Clive and Bonnie could assure Maude's safety and comfort. In truth, Bonnie was her mother-in-law's caregiver while Clive attended business meetings for most the day.

Maude had been living with her son and daughter-in-law for three years. She had experienced a series of small strokes called TIA's and due to an irregular heartbeat, a pacemaker had been implanted the previous year.

Bonnie had literally waited on Maude hand and foot to pacify her husband who demanded excellence for his mother without any notion of contributing to the efforts which would produce such excellence. Although Clive had not actually said anything to his wife about the recent stroke, Bonnie had concluded via Clive's silence and distance that she had somehow been remiss in Maude's care. In her husband's mind, she was responsible for Maude's present condition.

***

Tess, Bonnie and Clive proceed into the dining room. Ben skillfully manages to sneak to an adjacent table and snatch up a cookie from Will and Will shouts out his disapproval of Ben's success. Anita immediately takes Ben's hands and begins to sing him back to his own table while Clive gives a decided look of disapproval – or perhaps, it is disgust. Clive mouths to his wife, *They need to tie up that guy, not sing to him.*

Just as Connor raises his right foot to begin his compulsive trek across the dining room, Clive turns to approach the table where the balloon game is in progress. The two men bump shoulders. Connor looks frightened and he glares at Clive. Then, he turns and proceeds to strut across to the other side of the dining room.

Crazy, Clive utters as he goes to his mother's chair and touches her on the right shoulder. When she fails to turn around, Tess suggests he touch Maude on the left shoulder. When Clive complies, Maude immediately turns and produces a smile for her son.

Bonnie stands frozen a few feet away from her mother-in-law's table. She looks around, unable to comprehend the purpose of the activities and conversations going on all around her. She burps up acid and purses her lips to try to hold back years of negative feelings.

Thankfully, the uncomfortable moment passes and she goes to see Maude. Tess notices Bonnie's discomfort but she also knows that a first-time visitor may be put off by the seeming chaos of the House. Tess also knows that frequent visitors who want to understand the environment rather than simply relieve themselves of an obligation know that the seeming chaos is skillfully controlled, both by a talented staff and by state and federal laws. Tess will make no conclusions yet with Clive and Bonnie.

Tess suggests they all go into the family room. It is a smaller room with a couple of tables and a television set. The door can be closed so that the family can have privacy. The nursing station is just out the door and to the left. In case visitors need assistance, help is always close-by.

Tess offers to leave Maude, Bonnie and Clive alone but Clive immediately urges Tess to stay *In case my mother has questions about her stay here.* It seems to Tess that Clive might be frightened to be alone with a mother who now has *issues.* Clive puts on his brave face and asks, *So mother, how are things with you?* The corner of Tess's mouth begins to form a smile as she immediately asks the unresponsive Maude, *Have you been to physical therapy yet, Maude?*

Maude smiles and nods in the affirmative, holding up the index finger of her left hand. *Oh, one time already? That's great, Maude.*

And Clive then asks, *Well, how did that go for you, Mum?* When Maude struggles to talk, Tess intervenes, explaining that since Maude's speech is not yet *cooperating* with her, it is best to ask questions in which Maude can respond with gestures. Bonnie sputters and blurts out, **Oh, Mum, you're being so brave! We'll get you out as soon as we can!** Tears start to run down Maude's cheeks and Tess reaches for a box of tissues. She puts a tissue in Maude's left hand and Maude immediately dabs at her cheeks.

Fortunately for them all, Bill from physical therapy knocks on the door and comes in. **Ms. Maude, we are all ready for you now. It's time to get that hand back in the game. Here now, I'll just run you on down.** Bill apologizes to the relatives for taking Maude from them and says something about a *pretty tight schedule.* He takes the handlebars of Maude's chair and whisks her out of the room and down the hallway.

Tess takes the opportunity to escort Clive and Bonnie back to the office of the Admissions Director Trish Arnold, explaining there will be a lot of papers to sign. After the proper greeting all around, Trish hands a packet of material to Clive, explaining that all information regarding his mother's treatments in the facility will be included in the packet. She then produces a file of papers which Clive is required to sign so that his mother can be treated as a resident of the facility. Clive frowns and asks, *Now is everyone involved sure that this is the correct facility for my mother?* When Trish appears a bit taken aback, Clive follows with, *You know, it was all just so hurried and all.*

Remaining composed and cordial, Trish explains that there are many other suitable facilities in which Maude could receive treatment and that Clive is welcome to explore all options.

Apparently, Maude's placement had been one of bed availability combined with rehabilitation services available in the facility. But, Trish also stresses that they are pleased to have Maude with them and that the staff already considers her family. Clive bristles at a statement he considers far too familiar while Bonnie seems to concentrate on the remark for some personal meaning.

Then, Clive comments, *I noticed that the residents on my mother's unit seem to be a bit out of control. I would imagine that restraints are in order? My mother must be protected, of course.*

Trish explains that since October of 1990 facilities designated as *Skilled Nursing* can no longer use restraints to protect residents from harm to themselves or harm to others except in specific and extreme cases. She elaborates that restraints such as lap trays, Geri chairs, handmitts and tying the hands to beds or chairs are not allowed unless ordered by a physician to protect the resident from harm.

Trish then turns to a page in the packet she has given to Clive and she points to the paragraph which states that restraint by use of psychoactive drugs is also prohibited unless ordered by a physician.

Before Bonnie has the opportunity to ask, Trish says psychoactive drugs are medications that can alter moods and behaviors of residents and residents may appear drugged or sedated. Again, Trish explains that if such drugs are ordered, they are ordered to protect the wellbeing of a resident or the staff who work with that resident.

Clive and Bonnie become silent, both with looks of concern on their faces. So, Trish continues with information she offers to all new people every day. *Because restraints are only rarely used in the House, visitors are sometimes appalled by hearing residents shout or curse.*

Trish understands that the many visitors may be confused, frightened or repulsed by residents being allowed to pace the halls, talk gibberish and expose parts of the naked body. Some who had placed loved ones in the House had already volunteered to Trish and other staff members that the memory care unit reminded them of a scene right out of the movie *One Flew Over the Cuckoo's Nest*. But, Trish knows from experience that there are those who fail to notice the kindnesses and insights of the staff as they scurry to avoid potentially catastrophic incidents which might result in a resident needing to be restrained.

Those are the visitors who will need decorative trappings in more luxurious facilities to feel less guilt about placing a loved one. Trish looks at Bonnie and then, at Clive. She smiles while telling herself ***Poor Maude. She'll be transferred within a week.*** And, she was.

***

When Will's wife and Charlie's wife visit their loved ones in the House, they have rarely observed any use of restraints. Like Clive and Bonnie, they were also told during the admitting process that restraints could be used on Will or Charlie should the right circumstances arise. What the wives have observed is fascinating to them.

Instead of the use of restraints, the staff seems to simply change the environment so it appears less threatening to a resident. If Ben becomes agitated, he is led by the hands of Anita while she sings a soothing song and places him in a known position at his own table.

If Esther gets out of control verbally, Sharma may go to her and allow her to vent while distracting her in conversation such that she forgets a previous threat. When Leonard arises from his chair, risking a fall, Brianna will immediately grab his hands and dance with him back to the safety of his wheel chair. When Henry screams, he is assured that he is in a safe place and that his family is also safe.

No one in the house would even give momentary thought to remanding Millie as she saunters half naked down the hallway. Redirection always works with her. If someone cries, they are comforted. When Will demands to go home, his fears are heard and taken as real and legitimate. And, when Fred continually attempts to get out of bed, he is not restrained. Rather, he is given a sling-bed in which he may sink comfortably into the mattress, making it difficult to arise unless an aide is in the room to assist him.

Charlie's wife asked one day how staff was trained to be creative with residents rather than revert to the use of restraints. She was told that, in the House, the nursing staff has new staff members try on restraints and then tell how their freedom is restricted. They are trained to look for gestures such as stomping of the feet or showing of the fists as an indication that a resident wants to be removed from physician-ordered restraints.

Staff members look for facial expressions which suggest emotions that cannot be verbalized because of disease. If a resident does experience a fall, staff is trained to look at possible underlying conditions such as diabetes or low blood pressure. If such conditions are found, it is validation that restraints do not need to be used because of a potential fall risk. Rather, the underlying condition can be treated and the resident allowed maximum freedom of movement.

If a resident cannot get used to a wheel chair following previous upright mobility, aids such as dolls or furry toy animals can be clutched in the hands of the resident, making it difficult for a resident to use the hands to stand, thus risking a fall. Charlie's wife has frequently seen Gretchen holding a baby doll to her chest. Gretchen is both protective of the doll and loving toward the doll. Gretchen moves her feet to get around the halls and rooms of the house without risking using her hands to attempt to stand. And, many people ask Gretchen about the doll, providing ongoing opportunities for Gretchen to interact socially.

At the House, all staff members believe that if a restraint is viewed as punishment or it denies a resident access to movement or access to their own body, it is wrong. It may be convenient for the peace of mind of the staff, but it is wrong. There is no doubt that staff must spend more time in creative means of keeping residents safe but staff learning is evident in the wellbeing of those who trust their lives to those who work in the house of final release. And, because residents feel respected, they have given the gift of trust to their caregivers. These caregivers carry many scars from their learning. But, the scars only serve to remind them that learning comes at a cost. In the House, the cost is always the forfeiture of that which does not work.

***

"Scars are not signs of weakness, they are signs of survival and endurance."
Rodney A. Winters

CHAPTER TWENTY-TWO
Controlling Chaos

There are so many things that could go wrong in the House that it seems a miracle to many visitors that anything goes right. And yet it does. But on this day, things are going very wrong and there seems no end in sight.

Nearly a week ago, a new patient was admitted from another facility. It is common practice to screen all new admissions who could potentially infiltrate the facility and bring harm to residents through either physical and mental disorders or from infection. Vern underwent such screening and was admitted. It was not long before scabies was discovered among three residents, one of them being Vern.

Scabies mites are only detectable upon microscopic examination via skin scrapings. It is generally detected when an infected person begins to scratch the skin. Outbreaks of scabies, bedbugs and lice are most common in day care centers, schools, skilled nursing facilities and hospitals But, it can also occur in home care when visitors or healthcare professionals inadvertently bring in the infection. In a multibed-bed facility, an infectious outbreak will often bring general panic due to the time-consuming measures which must be taken to rid the victims and the environment of the mite.

When a single person is infected, it is generally treated with a topical ointment. Oral medication is also effective but it has potentially dangerous side effects for the geriatric population. Often, multiple treatments are necessary before the mite is eliminated.

Upon the first sign of disease, the House is forced to shut down the memory care ward and spring into action. All residents and staff are treated with the topical ointment which must be rubbed on all residents from head to toe. Extra staff is called in to treat the residents. For those with progressive dementia, it can be a frightening and frustrating experience. Visitors are not allowed into the unit and frequent visitors are told to monitor themselves for any suggestion of the infection. The CDC (Center for Disease Control) has laid out strict guidelines for treating infestations and the House is one of the top for compliance in the area. Nevertheless, the infection has shut down normal operations.

Following the twelve-hour ointment treatment, each resident is then showed. The treatment will be repeated in another week. In the meantime, all bedding, clothing and shower curtain material is disinfected and laundered. As strange as it may seem, most of the residents in the House are not terribly upset by the treatments and some enjoy the extra attention. It is a credit to the staff at the House that most residents remain unaffected. Beds must be disinfected as well as all furniture. It is literally a war, with staff being the soldiers and the mites the invading aggressors.

At the same time, Administration is tense because all procedures must be documented and reported to the State. They understand that all efforts to prevent being "cited" and becoming the subject of public report is now seemingly an effort in vain.

Following treatment measures, the memory care unit is

again opened and activities progress as usual. However, Administration is concerned about how the mite got into the unit and they explore all possible entry points. Eventually, it is discovered that one of Vern's visitors brought in the infection from outside. The House has no authority to screen visitors; thus, they are continually at risk.

*****

Another form of chaos may be experienced when multiple deaths occur. Since all of those at the House are considered terminal, death is inevitable. Under ideal conditions, the family of a newly admitted resident will have all papers in order. There will be a POA (Power of Attorney), a Health Surrogate will be named and an Advanced Directive will be included in the chart. The Advance Directive specifies what may be done at times when the resident is in a life-threatening situation.

In some situations, none of these papers are available in the resident's chart. If a resident stops breathing, a "code" will be called. The on-duty nurses will do their best until an ambulance arrives. With no advance directive, the paramedics have no choice but to continually attempt to revive the resident and then, transport to the hospital where revival attempts will be continued or the resident will be pronounced dead. If staff does not take measures to normalize such a situation, the noise and frantic activity can be very unsettling to residents. Generally, the door to the affected resident's room is closed and the roommate is removed to another room temporarily.

On one evening, Connor's wife was visiting when three residents received a code. Unfortunately, none of the residents had an Advance Directive and Staff was frantically attempting to meet the needs of all three victims while still maintaining order in the unit. Connor's wife stayed with her husband as he paced the halls and watched paramedics come and go. He appeared unaffected by the commotion, but many others were scared and they required comforting by various staff members. For nearly three hours, staff worked overtime trying to restore order to the unit. Many of the daytime staff stayed to assist victims and their families while the night staff began their work.

Two of the affected residents came back to the House later that night. Because of the trauma, it is likely they were even more damaged upon return. One did not return. Instead, his body was transported to a local funeral home. Shortly after that chaotic night, three family members of residents sought legal assistance to draw up Advance Directives for their loved ones. But, many did not. No one on staff got a medal that night; and there was no extra pay.

***

"If you're serious about sanctification, you can expect to experience heart-wrenching moments that try your faith, your endurance and your patience."
Sheri Dew, If Life Were Easy, It Wouldn't Be Hard

CHAPTER TWENTY-THREE
Flies in the Fan

It would be the last time in Charlie's lifetime that his wife would have a meaningful conversation with her husband. And, the conversational gift would remain with her for the rest of her life.

For well over three years, Charlie's wife had longed to converse with her brilliant, creative husband but the disease had won out day after day after day until she was convinced that a heartfelt verbal exchange was a thing of the past. But, on this day in the eleventh year of his disease, Charlie has a look in his eye that excites his wife and motivates her toward risk-taking. She accesses her own heart and encourages it through osmosis to enter the heart of her husband.

"Charlie, you are with me today."

At first, Charlie looks confused but ever-so-gradually, he produces a smile and answers, "Yes, perhaps."

"There is so much I want to know, Charlie" she says.

"Alright," he responds. Charlie reaches up his left hand. When it freezes in position, his wife lifts it to her cheek and gently strokes the cheek with Charlie's hand, much as Charlie had done throughout their decades of marriage. It is a simple thing, and yet. It is a connection of great intensity.

"What is it like for you, Charlie?" she asks.

"Bad," he says.

"How?" she asks.

"Flies in the fan," he says. "Always flies in the fan, for us all."

At first, she experiences confusion from the statement that appears non-responsive to her question. But then, she remembers when she and Charlie used to sit out on the lanai every night after dinner. In the summer, they always had the fan on and it was a peaceful, calming experience for them both. But then came the flies and they would fly right into the fan. On one evening, a mass of flies hit the fan and she had said, "Flies in the fan, Charlie."

And he had immediately replied, "And the frogs have a feast."

When realization of the context of Charlie's response registers in her brain, it is shocking! Charlie's wife envisions the flies being torn apart, their parts falling to the ground where they are consumed by the frogs. She gasps and holds back tears which fight hard to have their way. The images in her mind are ugly. In her brain, Charlie's thoughts are the flies hitting the fan. The thoughts are brutally torn to shreds and the pieces eagerly consumed by a group of opportunist frogs.

"Charlie, I..."

"Shhhh" he says and his hand slumps to his lap.

And then, Charlie's head slumps.

She knows he is having another silent seizure. It is as if he has foretold his experience verbally before he demonstrates behaviorally the hideous image of the flies hitting the fan. His thoughts and feelings appear to have been consumed in the current body spasms.

Charlie's wife waits it out while her own brain screams with a knowledge that can never again be unknown. In about twenty seconds, Charlie opens his eyes and tries to orient himself. He smiles when he sees his wife.

"Charlie?" she says.

"I have to go pee," he says.

"Charlie, you have a catheter and..." Then she stops and says, "I will get someone to help you."

"You can help me. You're a nurse."

And, *her* Charlie is gone for good this time.

***

She takes her husband to the nursing station and Jerri tells Charlie's wife she will put Charlie to bed for a nap.

***

"Perhaps we should not eagerly wish for tomorrow to come. It just might come to bite us in the butt."
        Author

CHAPTER TWENTY-FOUR
Charlie's Wife

The following day, Charlie's wife has a prominent feeling of apprehension when she is let inside the double locked doors. She has dressed carefully and she has brought a blueberry muffin for Charlie. She doesn't think the muffin or her careful attention to her own grooming will ward off the sense of doom that permeates her body on the way over.

Jackie tells Charlie's wife that her husband is outside in the butterfly garden. Charlie's wife apologizes for not being there to feed Charlie his breakfast and Jackie tells her it is not a problem as Charlie wasn't hungry anyway.

As she approaches her husband, Charlie's wife notes there are a multitude of butterflies today. They appear to be approaching Charlie and then, they fly away. Charlie stares at them with a sense of wonder as his wife gently touches his left arm. He turns toward his wife, attempts to reach out his left hand and then, he slumps.

At first, she thinks he has simply had another silent seizure. The episodes have been on the increase and Charlie's wife wonders how much more her husband's brain can endure before it yields to nothingness. She waits for half a minute and then tips up her husband's head. Generally, this motion will bring Charlie to a state of awareness. Instead, his head slumps back down

She talks to Charlie about the nearby residents and she comments on the butterflies. Still Charlie remains motionless. Jerri comes out to dispense medications. She attempts to rouse Charlie but he does not respond. His heart is beating and his breathing appears unobstructed but his head is slumped and his eyes are closed. Jerri finishes her medication rounds and comments on how deeply Charlie sometimes sleeps.

The butterflies appear drawn to Charlie and his wife. One of the small wonders of nature lands on her shoulder and another on Charlie's right hand. Charlie loves butterflies and yet, he simply will not open his eyes to look at the butterflies on this day. Barbara comes over and reaches out to Charlie with her unaffected left hand, commenting, *His brain won't let him open his eyes.*

Charlie's wife now has a fear that goes way past where her soul resides. She wheels Charlie back inside and directly to the nurses' station. She tells Jerri that she thinks Charlie has had *the big one.* She says they need to get him to bed and have him seen by the doctor.

Jerri immediately gets an aide and they take Charlie to his room and place him in bed. He does not awaken. Charlie's wife stays in her husband's room for some time, holding his hand and attempting to rouse him. Briefly, he opens his eyes and they are milky white and totally unaware. The eyes close again. She goes to the hallway and tells Jerri that she needs an assessment. Jerri understands what is required and she reports that the doctor can visit Charlie later that night or early in the morning. She tells Charlie's wife she needs to rest as *It may take a while.* Reluctantly, Charlie's wife turns to leave. In her professional role, she has attended many deaths and she knows the truth of Jerri's words.

***

The first thing in the morning, Charlie's wife returns and asks Jerri if the doctor has seen Charlie. Jerri answers that the doctor has seen no response whatsoever in Charlie. He says Charlie's breathing is shallow but even. Jerri tells Charlie's wife that Charlie has had a brain stem stroke. After a few more questions, Charlie's wife instructs Jerri to initiate Charlie's Advance Directive. Jerri nods and Charlie's wife goes to her husband's room to keep vigil.

She sits on the faded green chair with the scratched and worn wooden arms. She watches the form on the bed, with her own body so numb that it unfortunately allows all activity to be directed to her brain, where she ruminates about Charlie's condition. The images are horrible. She knows Charlie's brain is swelling. Pressure is rising in his brain, forcing the brain further down into the skull. Charlie is in a coma because of the pressure which will not allow the brain stem to rouse itself.

Unless Charlie is artificially nourished, his wife knows he is now on death watch. She agonizes between wanting Charlie to stay with her and honoring Charlie's wishes. She is grateful that she had the presence of mind to initiate the DNR (do not resuscitate) as she could just as easily rescind it were someone to ask about it at that moment.

Charlie's muscles are contracting under the tremendous assault to the brain. His legs are wrapped to try to prevent blood clots from forming. But, Charlie's wife knows the blood clots will have their way despite any kind of human intervention. Her mind flashes back to the day of her marriage to Charlie. There is no way to even try to contrast his young and vital body to that which lays seizing on the bed. She understood years ago this was the way it would end for Charlie. Nonetheless, it seems surrealistic.

Charlie's previous silent strokes and seizures have set him up for what has happened. The small strokes usually accelerate the process of death. It is a peculiar disease because it is one of the few illnesses which present little or no outward symptoms. Her own mind is now playing tricks. She hears the song she and Charlie danced to after their marriage and she chastises her brain for recalling such an intense image. She sobs openly, hoping no one comes in to witness the complete shattering of her soul. She is not embarrassed by her lack of composure. Rather, this is a private process, one in which she and Charlie must travel together. Surely, her gentle, brilliant, brave and creative Charlie deserves more grief than she could ever produce. She doesn't know if Charlie can hear her intense sense of desperation as she moans and attempts to stifle a total breakdown.

She doesn't know how she can get through this, so, she doesn't try. Charlie's wife simply allows the minutes to be what they are. Charlie sweats and his wife takes a cool, damp cloth and pats his forehead. He seizes and she holds his hands and strokes him and tells him he is very brave and she will see him through to his release. She tells him he gave her an exceptional life and at the same time, she cannot fathom a life without him.

During the seizures, Charlie sometimes grimaces. His wife cannot imagine what he must be enduring without the ability to seek help. She visualizes, eager, ugly frogs. As she strokes Charlie's arms, the seizures subside slightly and she can then get back to her story telling. She is relating the story of THEM. It is a story only the two of them can comprehend. She thinks maybe the story telling is helping to counter the seizures which appear to want to have their way with Charlie.

Charlie's wife fully understands that Nature will have her way. Nature is much more powerful than any treatment conceived by human beings.

***

"Sometimes, there's not a better way. Sometimes, there's only the hard way."
Mary E. Pearson, The Fox Inheritance

CHAPTER TWENTY-FIVE
Together We Stand

Charlie's wife has texted Will's wife about her vigil. Both women had expected Will to deteriorate first but apparently, Charlie's diseases had other notions.

It is still day two. Charlie cannot eat. He cannot swallow. He is bathed in bed and his body is soothed with lotion. Charlie's wife has asked for Hospice services. She does not want the comfort services of a Hospice agent. But, she knows the facility cannot administer morphine. She knows that Hospice has that privilege.

Despite medications, Charlie's seizures are increasing in intensity and duration. Charlie's wife cradles Charlie's head in her hand and attempts to stroke his spastic body. But, Charlie's heart continues to beat. His wife sings to him and she tells him stories about their decades together. She is not clear whether the singing and the stories are for Charlie or for her.

One-by-one, residents come to pay their respects to Charlie. They have noticed his absence in the dining room. Ben and Leonard come together in their wheel chairs. Ben verbalizes something and Charlie's wife thanks him for coming to see his friend. Leonard reaches out and touches Charlie on his leg and the leg momentarily stills itself. The Hospice worker comes in to check on Charlie and she is confused by the presence of the residents. She does not appear to understand what to do about their presence in a death room. So, Charlie's wife rises and tells the two men that it is time to go in for snacks now. She escorts the men out the door and up the hallway towards the dining room.

Charlie's wife is hungry but she does not want to leave her husband. Her son calls and she asks him to bring her something. Before long, he has come with a sandwich and a drink. He is nearly speechless. They both know this is the end but neither knows how it will end. No one teaches leaving because no one knows with any certainty just how another will leave life. The son leaves and Charlie's wife again begins to sing to her husband. She sings Always.

Before long, Esther comes to visit and she immediately takes the chair next to the one in which Charlie's wife is seated. She tells Charlie's wife that she has given orders to the staff and she hopes her orders are being carried out to the satisfaction of Charlie's family. This produces a genuine smile upon the face of Charlie's wife and she assures Esther that she is, indeed, doing a wonderful job directing the staff. Then, Esther comments that Charlie's mouth should be closed and she stands, seemingly to initiate the task herself. Charlie's wife intercedes, telling Esther that Charlie has a deviated septum and that his mouth must be open for him to take in air. Esther decides to exit, saying she will have the staff *bring in something for that leg shaking.*

She sits and ponders what is happening. No one has told the residents about Charlie's condition but Charlie's wife knows that they somehow sense Charlie's vulnerability. Most observers would be hard-pressed to acknowledge that there is a totally different but meaningful world in the hearts and minds of those residing in the House. Furthermore, it is a knowing mind.

Will's wife comes to sit with Charlie's wife. She will come, or go, as Charlie's wife wishes. She stays, and it is a comfort for Charlie's wife. The kindness will be returned in time.

In the evening, Charlie's daughter and son-in-law come in to visit. Charlie's wife understands that they have come to say good-bye. Charlie's daughter strokes him as the seizures come in waves. She and her husband both know that Charlie is processing something very intense and they are hard-pressed to know how to help him. But, they hold him and they talk to him and they tell him they love him.

A volunteer from the local American Legion comes into the room later in the evening. He salutes Charlie and thanks him for his service to his country. He puts a pin on Charlie's hospital gown and he has tears in his eyes as he places another pin on the shirt of Charlie's wife.

She stays very late that night. Her vigil is exhausting but she knows that Charlie is not yet ready to release. She cradles her husband's head and sings,

> *Days may not be fair, always*
> *That's when I'll be there, always*
> *Not for just an hour,*
> *Not for just a day,*
> *Not for just a year,*
> *But, always.*

Charlie's heartbeat slows and his breathing becomes slightly shallower. But, he does not release.

***

"Death comes in its own time."   *Charlie's Wife*

CHAPTER TWENTY-SIX
Closing In

It is the third day since Charlie succumbed to the stroke which has placed him in a coma. He continues his shallow breathing as life in the House continues around him. The Assistant Director of Nursing has brought in a cart. It contains things intended to soothe those who keep vigil over those attempting to release.

The cart contains a few snacks and bottles of water. There is a CD player and dozens of discs which contain messages of support. Charlie's wife places a disc on the player and pushes the button. The disc begins to play songs from decades ago. The songs bring tears to her eyes because old memories come in surges and she fears she will break into pieces before she can help Charlie to release. Finally, she turns off the music. Her task is difficult enough without being musically reminded of the decades of love, activity and passion she shared with her husband as imaged in the musical CD memory.

Jerri comes to check on Charlie and she again asks if she should close the door. Charlie's wife shakes her head and Jerri seems to understand that the natural rhythm of the House is somehow a comfort rather than a distraction for Charlie's wife. Jerri checks the leg compression elastic, turns Charlie on his side, and takes his vitals. The nurse is very efficient and she hopes that her various activities disguise the feelings of doom that her face projects every time she enters the room.

Charlie's wife has brought a book to read while she sits. Her eyes scan the words but there is no meaning to the story. Instead, she picks up Charlie's right hand and holds it in her own. She tells him it is okay to leave, to exit, to let go. He pays no attention to the words. Rather, he is invested in grimacing each time another seizure makes its way from his brain to the extremities of his body.

Barbara comes in and stretches out her left arm to Charlie's wife. She shakes her head, unable to verbalize her own feelings of loss for someone she has known so briefly. Barbara uses her good leg to propel herself to a place next to Charlie's wife. The two women hold hands. Charlie's wife hold Barbara's left hand as it is the only hand with feeling.

They sit in silence for twenty minutes. They both understand the requirements of grief. When Charlie's wife releases Barbara's hand to attend to Charlie's latest seizure, Barbara exits the room. Both women understand that their unspoken words have been well received.

Charlie's wife knows that Will's wife will be in today. She will take the medical transport with Will who has an appointment for a disability evaluation. Will has hearing aids and he may be eligible for monthly benefits as a veteran. After months and years of medical expenses, Will's wife will take any financial assistance for which she may be eligible.

The hearing evaluation is scheduled in a nearby community facility for 9:30 that morning. Will's wife has arrived over an hour early in case the transport comes early. But, by 8:45 am, the transport has still not arrived. Staff calls the service but no one is answering and Will's wife becomes more nervous with each passing minute. It is now almost 9:00 am and Will's wife decides to take things into her own hands. She is angry with herself that this appointment means so much, that the anticipation of a few more dollars a month is something so vitally important to her these days. But, she must stay the course and act on fact.

While Charlie's wife waits patiently for her husband to take his final breath, Will's wife grabs an aide from the dining room and asks her to help Will out to the front of the facility while she goes to get her car. While Charlie's wife sits mesmerized with the gradual intake and output of her husband's lungs, Will's wife scrambles to the car and drives it to the front entrance of the house. She leaves the motor running while she opens the trunk to accept Will's walker. While the aide secures Will in the front passenger seat, Will's wife jams the walker into the trunk and slams it shut.

Will is a flurry of questions and confusion. He keeps asking his wife where they are going and finally, in a moment of near panic, Will's wife asks her husband to cease talking. He complies for a moment, and then, he begins to ask again....and again. When his wife becomes lost in the unfamiliar environment, Will seems to pick up on her sense of disorganization and he escalates the frequency and urgency of his own need to understand why he is no longer in the House to which he has become accustomed.

At that same moment, Charlie's wife thinks her husband had accomplished his release. There is no rising of the chest and no open mouth in anticipation of taking in another supply of air for the lungs. She rises from her chair and goes to Charlie. She takes his right wrist and thinks she feels a faint pulse. She places her left cheek close to Charlie mouth and there is an ever-so-faint quantity of air being exhaled. Then, there is a gagging sound and Charlie's wife begins to sob, thinking *this is it*. And then, Charlie breaths again.

Will's wife stops at a gas station to ask for directions. There is no GPS in her car. She is from the generation in which getting lost and asking for directions is an established way of being. Having received directions from a patient gas station attendant, Will's wife calls the VA facility and tells them she is nearly there but will be slightly late. Will is quiet during the exchanges between his wife and the attendant and the VA facility and that draws instant praise for him from his wife.

Jerri comes in to turn Charlie and check his vitals. The seizures are continuing and Jerri asks Charlie's wife if she can administer more morphine. Charlie's wife cannot operate her mouth correctly so she nods her agreement.

Will and his wife make it to the hearing appointment only fifteen minutes late. Will's wife expects her husband to produce his most disorganized and negative behavior but he surprises her. The audiologist seems to anticipate that Will might be frightened about the change in his schedule and she talks with Will and gives him the respect he is due as a person who is simply trying to do his best under difficult circumstances.

Charlie's seizures slack in intensity but they continue throughout the day. While Will raises his hands to sound impulses, Charlie endures the relentless assault to his brain, followed by another and yet another. **Flies in the fan,** Charlie's wife thinks and she grimaces with the ugliness of her own mental images. Will's hearing exam consumes a half hour of his day. Charlie's release ordeal continues without abate.

Will's wife tells her husband he is going back to the House to have a snack and Will is delighted. When the car pulls up to the front door of the facility, Will comments that the place *looks familiar* and he willingly gets out of the car. Will's wife gets his walker from the trunk of the car and the two long-term lovers walked together to the front door where they are met with a smile by a staff member. Will eagerly walks inside the House while his wife gets back into the car and drives back to a world which is far more gentle and kind than the world in which Charlie's wife continues to keep vigil.

***

"All we have to decide is what to do with the time that is given us."
J.R.R. Tolkien, The Fellowship of the Ring

CHAPTER TWENTY-SEVEN
Falling In

In the House, it is not unusual for one death to follow another. And, this period is no different from any other time. Residents are not sheltered from events; rather, those events are a natural course of the day. Most residents conclude that the paramedics will be available for others but will never need to come for them personally.

Dancing Leonard has been frail for many, many months and yet, it is his wife who has now succumbs. Her caregiving years have simply cost her too much and now, her body cannot endure the sole task of self-care. Henry released himself from his affliction the previous evening and the paramedics were unable to restart his heart. Although she is not among the afflicted, Leonard's wife is among the fallen. Leonard does not notice the absence of his wife as normal activities continue throughout the day. For many months to come, Leonard will carry on with the belief that his wife visits him daily. And, who is to say that Leonard's belief is not the truth.

When Charlie's wife hears the news about the death of Leonard's wife, she is filled with grief but she has no time to grieve for a fallen comrade. She understands that she also is vulnerable to death but that kind of thought has no room in a mind bent on helping a husband to release.

It is the fourth day of the vigil and little has changed. Charlie's wife has a heart that is pregnant with the knowledge that her husband is unable to let go of a life he cherished. His passion was what endeared him to his wife, his family and his friends. And now, that passion has become his arch enemy. Charlie's brain knows better than to linger. It was a topic of discussion between he and his wife on many occasions. But now, Charlie needs something elusive, something other than his own belief so his wife searches her mind for answers. She experiences one failure of cognitive creativity after another. She has helped her husband through a failing body and a failing mind for nearly eleven years now. And now, when it counts, she feels helpless at the most critical moment of her husband's life.

Her mind flashes to the last evening of their vacation to Italy. It was ten years ago and she understood at the time that the vacation might be their last. Charlie had not yet accepted his own failing, so his wife acknowledged the fact for both. And then, that last night in Rome, Charlie had told her he had known all along.

They were in a restaurant and had finished their meal. Charlie insisted on coffee and dessert, so they shared a delicious Italian delicacy. When only cake crumbs were left on the plate, Charlie took his wife's hand in his and he began to sing;

"Besame, besame mucho,
Como si fuero esta noche
La ultima vez."

Charlie's wife immediately recognized the lyrics as those of Mexican songwriter Consuelo Velasquez who wrote the famous bolero in 1940. It had always been a favorite of hers. She silently translated the lyrics to English:

"Kiss me more, kiss me much more times
As if this beautiful night
Is the very last time.

Kiss me more, kiss me much more times
Because I fear I will lose you
I'll lose you sometime.

I want to have you right by me
To look at me in your eyes
And see you beside me.
I think that maybe tomorrow
I'll be away far,
Far from where you'll be."

On that night, Charlie had sung the entire song in Italian while tears flowed down his wife's face. They both understood what was being acknowledged and it cemented them in knowledge and fused them in solidarity for the challenge of years yet to come. The fact that Charlie knew he was failing and that he understood how fate would so cruelly change their relationship was almost too much for his wife to bear. And so, she simply sat and smiled her love and her commitment.

When Charlie had stopped singing, the other diners had clapped in appreciation of yet another love story in the city of Rome. The restaurant manager came to the table and said there would be no charge for the meal as Charlie had provided free entertainment to the diners. It had been a truly magical night of revelation which would propel Charlie and his wife to the present task of releasing Charlie from life.

And now, Charlie's wife talks with her son as she nibbles on the sandwich he has brought. She can see the urgency on the face of her son. He wants Charlie to release so that his mother can be spared even more intense pain and possibly, her own life. He sees the stress on her face and now, she is heavy with grief.

Ben and Leonard again come in, Leonard looking at Charlie with an expression of intense curiosity. When they leave, Esther arrives, wanting assurance that Charlie is receiving the best possible care from *her* staff. Charlie's ordeal has provided a wonderful delusion in which Esther can feel efficacious and valued.

Charlie's wife waits for everyone to leave and then, she decides that this moment may just be the moment Charlie needs. She has brought the words with her on a piece of paper and she begins to sing softly:

"Besame, besame mucho"

Charlie does not seem to react. But, when his wife tops singing, a tear has trickled down his right cheek and Charlie's wife thinks she might have found the key to helping break through the vicious cycle of seizures racking her husband's body and brain. She feels momentary relief. *Tonight*, she thinks to herself, *tonight will be the night of his release.*

For six minutes, Charlie's body is calm and relaxed. And then, the seizures begin. When Jerri comes in to say she will be leaving for the night, she sees the tense and drawn expression on the face of Charlie's wife and she pulls out the medication. Charlie's wife gives a nod of approval, unable to face the thought that the medication may accomplish what she cannot.

***

"When he shall die,
Take him and cut him out in little stars,
And he will make the face of heaven so fine
That all the world will be in love with night
And pay no worship to the garish sun."
William Shakespeare, Romeo and Juliet

CHAPTER TWENTY-EIGHT
Business as Usual

There is no more shouting from Henry today but Esther again believes that Connor is her personal body guard. The dining room has been cleaned from breakfast and is now prepared for the next activity.

Some will take morning naps and others will attend activities. Louie and Will sit at a table together deciding whether the Navy or the Army salute is superior.

Annie comes into the dining room with her husband who walks gingerly with his cane, looking more and more drawn and defeated. He tries to talk with his wife but he cannot get to the place where she now resides. It is business as usual.

It is the fifth day of the vigil for Charlie's life and Charlie's wife. It is not business as usual for her and the staff at the House is fully aware of the strain in the generally-composed woman. For decades, the staff has attended to hundreds of people like Charlie's wife and they have also attended to those in the House with totally different needs. And, that is why the House has remained functional and strong.

Charlie's wife has slept precious little and she looks exhausted. She has used all her professional and personal skills to try to relate to where Charlie might be in the process of release.

Charlie has been sponge-bathed and shaved. He is in a clean hospital gown, with pillows propped under his legs. His mouth is slightly open and his breathing is shallow but regular.

Seizures continue to move his arms and his legs and each time he spasms, his wife goes to him, cradles his head and speaks to him. She then goes to rub the limbs which now serve no purpose other than to transmit nonfunctional electrical impulses.

Jerri comes in to deliver medication intended to lessen the seizure activity. She also looks drawn and concerned.

The nurse does not understand what is keeping Charlie in the living world and she can see the stress on the face of Charlie's wife. Jerri wants all of those under her care to go gently into the good night. But, that rarely happens.

Death has its own course of action and that course is as different as the individuals it affects are unique.

Charlie's wife can hear residents moving up the hallway toward the dining hall. It is now snack time and unless they are in a deep, oblivious sleep, those who reside in the House do not miss snack time. There are random thoughts coming to her now and they seem to fire much as the seizures fire in Charlie's brain. It is almost as if she and Charlie are now in a synchronous, chaotic, parallel process.

She thinks about all the roles Charlie has played in his life and how well he functioned in those roles. He was son, brother, friend, student, athlete, Navy Lieutenant, Doctor, Professor, colleague, mentor, fisherman, hunter, intellect, avid reader, conservationist, administrator, husband, lover, grandfather. Charlie's wife thinks there are many, many more roles in Charlie's life but they do not come to mind at that moment.

After the passing of the next seizure, Charlie's wife has a lightning bolt idea of her own. She must go to where Charlie is *now*. She has been relating to him as a wife, companion and friend and he is no longer in those roles. She must find where he is and she must go there and help him to release.

Her mind rehearses the past month and how Charlie had interpreted his environment in the House. Although he appeared to know their relationship prior to the stroke, he was already in a different place.

He told her that. He told her he was in the Navy in so many ways. He talked about being a spy and he talked about guiding his destroyer into Guantanamo Bay during the Cuban Missile Crises. Charlie had saluted her and he had saluted many of the staff as well. And, they had saluted back, nice, crisp salutes intended to pay Charlie the respect to which he was entitled.

Charlie's wife knows his body will die soon without nourishment. But, he had always expressed the desire to participate in his own death and she wants so very much for that to be his final experience of life. It will be an intimate act of love. She finally knows exactly what to do.

Before Charlie's wife can act on her instincts, she hears a general commotion outside. She goes to the door and sees four staff members running to the dining area. And then, the hallway goes still. She walks up the hallway to the dining room and sees two nurses attending to Louie. They are transferring him from his chair to a wheel chair. Louie is awake or, at least, his eyes are open. But, he appears disoriented and somewhat fearful.

Louie is taken down to his bedroom and the residents are served snacks. Within seconds, the incident with Louie is forgotten by those living in the House. Not only is a poor memory a great coping mechanism in the House, it is a reality which prevents most residents from remembering from moment to moment. Charlie's wife shakes her head and heads back down to Charlie's room.

She has an important task at hand and Charlie's wife knows it may very well be the most tender and critical moment of life with her husband. She waits for the next seizure to pass as she strokes Charlie's arms and his legs. She lifts her husband's head and she kisses him gently on the forehead and then on both cheeks. His skin is moist and hot, or maybe, that's her skin. As she begins to speak, Jerri walks quietly into the room and she stands at the foot of the bed, careful not to intrude in such an intimate moment.

With tears streaming down her face, Charlie's wife says; *Lieutenant Douglas, this is your commanding officer. You have gone above and beyond the call of duty to your family and your country. You are officially discharged from duty. Lieutenant Douglas, release yourself.*

Ever-so-gently, Charlie's wife places her husband's head back on the pillow. She kisses Charlie's forehead and she then goes to her chair to wait. She is weak and she feels she might fall on the floor if her body is not supported. By the time she is safely in the cushioned seat, Charlie's body has gone completely still.

Jerri goes to Charlie, takes his pulse and says his heart continues to beat. But Charlie's body is now still. And, there are no more seizures. Jerri has tears in her eyes but she smiles gently at Charlie's wife. They are both at peace now. Time will have its way.

***

"I do not fear death. I had been dead for billions and billions of years before I was born. I was born, and had not suffered the slightest inconvenience from it."

Mark Twain

"You gained and you lost, and if you saved anything from the ruins, even if only a shred of self-respect, it was enough to take you through the next bit."

Dick Francis, Whip Hand

CHAPTER TWENTY-NINE
Release

Jerri picks up the medication and Charlie's wife nods. The morphine is placed under Charlie's tongue. It will slow Charlie's heartbeat and his heart will expend itself. As she leaves the room, Jerri touches Charlie's wife on the shoulder. Charlie's wife says a choked *Thank you* and she is then alone.

No one comes in as Charlie's heart continues to beat. The heart beat without Charlie's knowledge during the first weeks of conception and, even though he is released and unaware, it will have its way now as well. There is water to drink and Charlie's wife also has a sandwich she cannot eat.

A Hospice worker comes in and sees the situation is well in hand and she leaves Charlie's wife to her own thoughts because she understands that is what Charlie's wife wants.

Others want conversation and assurance at times like these, but Charlie's wife is a private person. No one teaches leaving, but Charlie's wife is content knowing she has helped her husband to release. And she is now very grateful to her husband who is teaching her the art of leaving.

In the late afternoon, Will's wife comes in and is surprised to see Charlie's body still and free of seizures. On several occasions, Charlie's wife checks his pulse as does Jerri when she comes in. Charlie's wife explains what she has done to help Charlie to release and Will's wife says she hopes she can be strong as well. It is hard for Charlie's wife to see Will's wife struggle. They have become friends and Charlie's wife knows that her journey with Charlie is nearly at an end but that her friend's husband may struggle for months, or even, for years. The women talk and then, Will's wife says she must go. She goes to Charlie and kisses him. And then, she leaves.

Jerri comes in to tell Charlie's wife it is the shift change and she introduces Elizabeth, the night nurse. Charlie's wife thinks for a moment and then, she tells Elizabeth that she has told Charlie good-bye. She is of the belief that her heart is so firmly merged with that of her husband that, if he knows she is there and can hear her voice, his heart will not cease to beat. Elizabeth nods her understanding and Charlie's wife leaves the building. She knows there will be a phone call, probably as soon as she arrives at home.

She must wait when she gets into her car. It is hot and she turns on the ignition to get the air conditioner going. Charlie's wife is sobbing and she knows she cannot drive. Her son and daughter have told her to call but she will wait until she gets the call from Elizabeth. She knows she can do this. It is part of the leaving and part of the learning. She waits in the car until the sobbing and tremors have ceased and then, she pulls out of the driveway, drives on the side road and waits at the busy intersection for the light to change.

Charlie's wife is very careful. She knows she is a compromised driver. She is compromised with grief, with finality. And yet, she feels a freedom she has not felt for the past decade. She feels happy for Charlie. He has endured and now, the final victory over life will soon be his. They only need to untangle their hearts so that Charlie's heart can cease to beat while hers continues.

On the way home, she stays in the right lane and goes under the speed limit. She begins to focus on all the wonderful memories instead of the bad times. She sees the trip to the Bahamas where they snorkeled and the Cayman Islands where they recklessly celebrated their love for one another. As she approaches her house, she stops in the road, just shy of her driveway. She swears she sees Charlie in front of her. They are on the mountaintop together in Italy. His left hand is extended as he beckons her to go down the other side of the mountain – alone. It is understood that they have climbed the mountain together, and that only she will go down the other side. She knows her heart is now her own.

She pulls into the driveway and secures the car. Charlie's wife goes into the house to get a drink of water when her cell phone rings. She sees the caller ID and she answers, saying *He's gone, isn't he?*

Elizabeth says she didn't want to be the one to call and Charlie's wife says it is okay. Elizabeth asks if Charlie's wife wants to come back and Charlie's wife says *We have said good-bye.* There is more conversation which Charlie's wife will not remember.

"I go to seek a Great Perhaps."   *Francois Rabelais*

CHAPTER THIRTY
Annie's Husband

The next day, Charlie's wife is making phone calls when Annie's husband goes to the House to visit. He can barely navigate the hallways and those who know him understand that the emotional baggage he carries is proving to be too great a burden.

Lately, Annie's husband stays in Annie's room while Annie wanders. She vacillates moods rapidly now and the changes are overpowering to her husband. For a brief minute, she displays a long-held intelligence that drew her husband to her. But, those moments are now rare and instead, Annie has adopted a shrew-like presence that scares her husband. She may have no awareness of her own presentation or it may be that the moods reflect the companionship she has lost. Annie's room is intended to be a place of solace for her. But now, her husband hides there for safety.

Anyone with an eye open to reality can surmise that Annie's husband will be among the sixty percent of caregivers who will die before their loved one. And as foretold, it is not long before Annie's husband fails to come to the house. His daughter who lives up north has been called to come and care for him. His frailty will lead to death and who is to say that Annie's husband has not been granted his wish.

*****

It is a choice to participate in the death of a loved one. No one is more and no one is less noble based upon what they choose. But to choose not to choose – is certainly a fatal decision by any measure of the choice.

***

"Often you shall think your road impassable, somber and companionless. Have will and plod along and round each curve you shall find a new companion."
Michal Naimy, The Book of Mirdad

CHAPTER THIRTY-ONE
Collections

The morning after Charlie's death, his wife and daughter drive to the House to pick up Charlie's scant belongings. Charlie's wife had instructed the night nurse to donate all clothing to the House as there were some residents who had no means to buy clothing

The two women go to the memory care nursing station and Jerri immediately comes out from behind the desks to hug Charlie's wife. There is little to be said. Residents look at Charlie's wife but they do not approach her on that day. Their understanding seems both natural and uncanny.

Jerri hands a box of belongings to Charlie's daughter and a plastic sack to his wife. His belongings include Charlie's Navy blanket, several pictures, Charlie's wallet and identification and a pillow with the picture of the grandchildren imprinted on it.

Every night since he had been at the house of final release, Charlie had been put to bed and covered with the Navy blanket. He would then be handed the pillow and he would tuck it under his left arm and keep it close to his heart all night.

Charlie's wife and daughter go to the double doors and are let out. Sharma and Anita wave and blow kisses to them as they exit to the front hallway.

In the hallway, they are met by Stacey and she immediately expresses her condolences as does the receptionist Brianna. Stacey is attending to a woman in a wheel chair. The woman stares at the plastic bag and then says **You have my pillow.**

The plastic bag is tightly tied and Charlie's wife is eager to exit the building. She looks at Stacey and Stacey shrugs as if to say she knows nothing about the woman's statement. Then, the woman says **I made that and I'd like to have it back.**

Charlie's wife knows nothing about a pillow other than the pillow with the grandchildren's faces imprinted on it. She needs to leave. So, they do. That afternoon, Charlie's wife attempts to arrange for Charlie's military service at the national cemetery in the city in which they live. But, arrangements remain in limbo as others call and email, all wanting information.

It isn't until the following morning that Charlie's wife opens the cardboard box of belongings. She puts away the pictures and the wallet and other small personal possessions. Then, she opens the bag containing the pillow with the picture of the grandchildren. Beneath Charlie's pillow, there is another smaller pillow. It is a patchwork design and it looks decidedly homemade. It may well belong to the woman in the hallway, attended to by Stacey.

How the pillow had made its way into Charlie's meager possessions is beyond the comprehension of Charlie's wife. But, on occasion, things do go missing. Neither of Charlie's two pair of eyeglasses is among his possessions.

Charlie's wife was told that there was a woman who collected eyeglasses from around the facility and she kept them in a drawer in her room. None of the staff had any notions why Ginny collected the eyeglasses, but her room was the first place they looked when eyeglasses went missing.

Charlie no longer needs his eyeglasses. But, his wife will take back the pillow. Who knows what memories are sewn into the patchwork? Perhaps, they span the lifetime of the woman who asked for the pillow.

***

"A man may die, nations may rise and fall, but an idea lives on. Ideas have endurance without death."
John, F. Kenned

CHAPTER THIRTY-TWO

Billie Joe and Tonto

Will's wife tells Charlie's wife that Will has a new roommate but Will has not noticed the man. The new roommate is frequently accompanied by a visitor. The roommate seems to know the visitor.

The man who accompanies Will's new roommate tells Will's wife that his friend's name is Billie Joe and that he is a musician. Billie Joe's friend is named Sam. Sam is some type of manager. He tells everyone who will listen that Billie Joe has played his violin all around the world and that Billie Joe is part of a duo.

Sam tells Will's wife that the other musician is called Tonto. His real name is Antonio but he has always gone by the nickname of Tonto. The man is Spanish-American and he plays a Spanish guitar.

Will's wife wonders how a violin and a Spanish guitar can entertain a crowd for hours so Sam tells her to go to the internet and Google Billie Joe and Tonto. Sam says they write their own music and Will's wife is impressed by that. Will's wife notes that Billie Joe has a strange presentation, with out-of-focus eyes.

She thinks she has seen others who look like that. They use drugs and have fried their brains. But then, dementia will do that to you as well, she concludes.

When she gets home that night, Will's wife Googles Billie Joe and Tonto. Several videos pop up and Will's wife chooses one of them to watch. She thinks the musicians are very good. She chooses another video and on that one, she swears she sees Billie Jack reaching over for a cannabis bong. She now has a hypothesis related to Billie Joe's medical condition. But, who is she to judge? The videos are pleasing and Will's wife thinks it a shame that Tonto now plays all over the world without Billie Joe.

That night, Will's wife gets a call from the House. Will's new roommate has hit Will and no one has a clue why. Will used to be able to give a ready presence of combativeness and intimidation but that look has not been available to him for some time now. Will's wife doesn't like the sound of it. She silently vows to consider some action before things get out of control. She used to be a bit wary of her own husband but now, she is the one in control and he is the one who is scared.

Two days later, Will's wife waits for the double steel doors to open. She glances into the unit and sees Will at a table. He is alone today. When the doors are unlocked for her, Will's wife goes to the nursing station and she sees Letti. Lettie immediately tells her that Billie Joe has again gone after Will. No one can figure out what the problem is as there are never any witnesses. Will's wife says in an affirmative voice that she does now. Will is assigned a new roommate that evening.

Will is no longer bothered if his wife does not come to visit. In fact, he never asks for her. At first, it bothers her and then, over dinner one night, Charlie's wife says it is a tribute to Will's sense of belonging that he is content to be part of the House. Will's wife thinks over the comment and she decides it is a positive way to think.

Will's wife comments that Charlie's military service was highly moving and Charlie's wife thanks her for the validation that will move her toward life as a single woman. Will's wife inquiries about what has been done following Charlie's death.

Charlie's wife says it is best to get everything in order before a death as there is much to do afterwards. There are so many people and companies to notify. **Mostly, the calls are okay,** Charlie's wife says. But then, she says she is disgusted that she had to bring Charlie's death certificate to Comcast to get her name put on the contract agreement. Charlie's wife was born in a time of mutual trust in business and she thinks a phone call should have sufficed.

For a couple of weeks now, Will has had a troublesome rash and no one seems able to get it under control. A dermatologist is called in and a new suave is ordered. Will's wife goes to pick up the ointment that may soothe her husband and is told by the pharmacist that Medicaid will not cover the medication.

She calls the House and is told that another medication may work just as well, so Will's wife picks up the medication and takes it to Lettie on her next visit. Will's wife thinks it is a strange medical system that allows a person with a certain amount of money to get a recommended medication while someone with not quite as much money must settle for second-best. But, if the suave does the job, she will not complain.

During the current visit, Will's wife notices that Esther is not in the dining room for lunch. In fact, she was not there during the last visit either. Will's wife inquiries about Esther and is told she is having a rough time and she stays a lot in her room these days. Will's wife is told not to worry as Esther has done this in the past.

Hmmm... Will's wife thinks. **Strange how the absence of just one person can change the dining room dynamics.** But then, Ben comes over to steal Will's coffee and Anita takes his hands and sings him back to him table and Will's wife thinks that things haven't changed all that much.

Will's wife looks around the dining room and notes that Louie is absent from Will's table. She asks Sharma if Louie is okay and she is told that Louie has had a stroke. He can speak but his movements are labored and he spends a lot of the day sleeping now. Will's wife shakes her head and thinks how quickly a human life can change. She asks about Leonard's wife and Lettie just shakes her head. Another caregiver has been lost.

Will's wife is getting frightened. Just when she thinks everyone is stable in the house and the caregivers have a reprieve, the stress gets them anyway. She will go for a long walk tomorrow and toughen up her own heart.

***

"It's not that we have to quit this life one day, it's how many things we have to quit all at once, holding hands, hotel rooms, music, the physics of falling leaves, vanilla and jasmine, poppies, smiling, anthills, the color of the sky, coffee and cashmere, literature, parks and subway trains.
Roman Payne – Hope and Despair

CHAPTER THIRTY-THREE
Charlie's Wife

Charlie's wife has now known Will's wife for close to a year and she is amazed at how mutual pain and circumstances has made them good friends. Will's wife helped Charlie's wife through the process of Charlie's death and now, Charlie's wife will assist Will's wife through the continuation of Will's life.

It is nearly Christmas and Charlie has been gone for six months now. Will's wife will go north to be with her family for the holiday so Charlie's wife volunteers to look in on Will during her absence. She thinks it may be a good idea to pop into the House unannounced during the holiday absence, just to make sure Will is being attended to properly.

Charlie's wife thinks it will be strange to go back to the House, but she also thinks she will be alright. She wonders if she will view things differently in the House now that she no longer has a loved one there.

Upon entering the House, Brianna greets Charlie's wife like a long-lost friend. The feelings of welcome are genuine and Charlie's wife relaxes and proceeds to the memory care unit. When she is inside the locked doors, she goes to the nursing station to inquire about Will.

Jerri is either off work that day or attending to residents. Lettie tells Charlie's wife that Will is about the same. *But he has failed some since you were last here,* she adds. Charlie's wife goes to the dining room and looks for Will. At the very moment she spots Will, Barbara comes up to her in the wheelchair, holding out her left hand.

Charlie's wife is stunned that Barbara remembers her. She kneels to make eye contact with Barbara and she begins to talk. It is not one of Barbara's better days. Barbara tries to talk but then, she begins to cry. Charlie's wife simply gives her a hug and Barbara wheels herself back to her table. It appears that Barbara is getting used to the betrayals of her brain and she has learned to go back to the known.

Will smiles at Charlie's wife, although he probably does not remember who she is. His speech has deteriorated since Charlie's death and Charlie's wife must put forth considerable effort to hold a conversation. Will's walker remains at his side as he is seated in a dining chair. Charlie's wife wonders how long before Will is confined to a wheelchair.

While Will eats his lunch, Charlie's wife looks around the room and she spots several new residents. Many of the residents who were there with Charlie seem unchanged. She sees Marilyn's son sitting with her for their daily luncheon get-together. Marilyn cannot talk but her son keeps up a conversation and both mother and son seem to benefit from the exchange. Charlie's wife likes the interaction and she smiles. Sometimes, goodness just deserves a smile of appreciation.

She has more time now to study interactions between the staff and the residents, so Charlie's wife takes her time. She has noticed before how residents oftentimes speak with behaviors but this time, she truly notices how responsive staff is to alternative ways of expressing their needs.

With some residents, physical touch is an essential means of communication. With others, disruptive behaviors express feelings of need and belonging which are unable to be verbalized. Most of the needs seemed to be basic needs for food and safety but on occasion, higher order needs such as social inclusion needs would be expressed in unorthodox ways.

For a moment, Charlie's wife tries to recall when her own behaviors toward Charlie underwent change. Ever since the moderate disease state, she and Charlie had been in somewhat a synchronous rhythm, much like the residents and staff of the House. It wasn't until Will shouts, *Shut up!* to a resident across the table that Charlie's wife remembers the unusual way she would relate to Charlie. She calmly says, *Will likes to concentrate on his meal, Bart.* With that simple reply, her own behavioral changes are remembered.

Even though it had been six months since she'd interacted with Charlie, she immediately recognizes need behaviors again. She smiles at Bart and he seems to forget how to respond.. She instantly recognizes that Will needs to concentrate on bringing the fork to his mouth and that Bart's chatter is disrupting his ability to carry through with the sequence of the motion.

Will can no longer talk and carry through with the process of eating simultaneously. His shouting is now his most effective means of communicating his need. There is no multitasking among residents in the House. It is a simple rule that is violated daily when visitors arrive to chat with loved ones.

Charlie's wife understands many things now. Prior to Charlie's death, they had previously been unknown simply because she was actively in the caregiving process. She now knows that she grew closer to Charlie and was better able to react to his needs when she had let go of who Charlie *was* and simply interreacted with who he had become. That is a behavior that eludes many caregivers as they continue to wish for what was. Since the staff at the House had never interacted with the residents as they *were*, it seemed more natural for them to attend to the behavior that expressed current, unfulfilled needs.

Anita was no longer in the dining room. She was such a bonus to the operation of the noon meal as well as the afternoon activities. But, Anita was on maternity leave and Jackie had stepped up to fill her shoes. Charlie's wife also missed the presence of the Activities Director who had been an integral part of the daily operations of the House.

Charlie's wife now wonders how many more staff could be lost before the dynamics of the residents and staff would suffer. Staff turnover was a problem in any organization dependent upon cooperation and cohesion. She ponders about the glue that holds things together in the House.

She is jolted from her thoughts when Will says, *So, how about a kiss before you go?* He then follows with, *Or we can have sex too!* Charlie's wife immediately understands that Will has mistaken her for his wife. She smiles and says *Thanks, Will. It is time for me to go. Your wife says I may kiss you on the forehead and she sends her love.* Will is perfectly content with the friendship kiss and he has no comprehension that he has provided vital information to Charlie's wife in the process.

That evening, Charlie's wife texts Will's wife that everything is fine and that Will sends her his love. Will's wife texts back asking if he *really* said that. Charlie's wife texts back that Will *is* just fine and Will's wife texted, *Thanks, thought so.*

***

The following day, Charlie's wife calls Habitat for Humanity and asks if they may be interested in the donation of a brown leather sectional. The sectional is only two years old. Charlie's wife had taken Charlie shopping for something more comfortable for her husband and he had loved that boring sectional. He had pleaded for his wife to get it for him. Charlie's wife had yielded because Charlie never asked for anything anymore. For six months after Charlie's death, every time she looked at the sectional, she visualized Charlie with one struggle after another. She visualized him playing with his "busy blanket," a small quilt intended to pacify and occupy young children.

She could not get past the images of Charlie on the sectional. She finally concluded that the sectional was impeding her ability to replace the more recent negative images with the positive images of her years with her husband.

After having visited the House the previous day, she is finally able to see how changes occur after she is no longer involved in the action. She is no longer a caregiver or an advocate. Charlie no longer needs the sectional. She is a single person and she has the right to make her house her home.

Two men from Habit for Humanity come two days later. They disassemble the sectional. They tell Charlie's wife that the sectional is in like-new condition and will probably be placed in one of their new homes, a family home. When the last section is carried from the house, Charlie's wife puts her left thumb to her mouth and bites the nail.

Good-bye, Charlie struggles, she silently says. And then, she has the presence of mind to say to the two men, *Thank you so much.* Charlie's wife thinks to herself how strange it is that total strangers can oftentimes figure into the complicated machinations of healing. With a simple act, she will now begin another journey of her own.

"When you stop growing, you start dying."
William S. Burrough

CHAPTER THIRTY-FOUR
Will's Wife

It seems to Will's wife that months have passed since she last visited the House. Will has not asked once about his wife during her absence. For Will's wife, it was a mixed blessing. She is relieved that Will is now a member of the House community. On the other hand, she wonders if there is still a place for her in her husband's life.

When she goes to his room, Will's wife is greeted with a smile from her husband and he says, *Oh, there you are,* as if he'd been looking for her like a recently misplaced item. She bites her lip and begins to scrutinize Will's appearance. Other than needing a haircut, Will's wife surmises that her husband has fared well in her absence.

Lettie tells Will's wife that Will is now falling frequently and she suggests Will might be ready for a wheelchair. Will's wife has no objection but, like everything else, a wheelchair will be a change. And, Will does not handle change well at all.

For the first time since Will's admittance to the Memory Care Unit of the House, Will's wife decides to allow staff to handle that transition.

After a short visit, Will's wife goes to talk with the Administrator about recent staff changes. She is told that there will soon be a new Director of Nursing and a new Activities Director. Then, the Administrator unloads a bombshell. She tells Will's wife that she will soon be retiring. Feelings of uncertainty begins to seep through the cells of Will's wife's brain.

Old feelings of fear and inadequacy begin to permeate her skin. She has worked so hard to get Will to accept his new environment and now, that environment is about to do a one hundred and eighty degree turn.

She decides not to comment. Will's wife will text Charlie's wife and get some input before becoming unraveled. She is learning and the learning feels like a settling force in which she takes comfort.

***

Following several back-and-forth texts that evening, Will's wife learns something about herself. Charlie's wife has suggested that Will's stability comes from those directly involved in his care and that he may not even notice a change in staff with those he sees infrequently. And so, Will's wife decides to wait and to observe.

***

Will's wife develops an infection that seems to resist antibiotics. After an initial period of recovery, she is told she may again visit the House but that she should not go into the Memory Care Unit. There is a window in the large dining room that allows her to keep track of Will's progress without going through the locked doors.

As she approaches the locked doors, Will's wife notes that the old doors have been replaced and now, they are freshly painted. The old doors contained transom windows that allowed taller visitors to peek in before entering. But, the new doors have a film over the windows, preventing viewing of the hallway. At first, Will's wife is alarmed. But then, she reasons that the privacy of the residents is being protected from those who are merely curious, and she smiles in agreement of the decision.

It has been two weeks since Will has transitioned to the wheelchair and for the most part, he has accustomed himself to the new means of mobility. But on occasion, he will rise, forgetting that he can no longer safely transport himself from one location to another.

Will's wife immediately spots her husband. He is seated in a regular chair at his dining table. Suddenly, Will rises and begins to walk. He is hunched over and struggling to navigate. Will's wife looks in horror as Will continues to shuffle on past staff who are attending to others. Will proceeds toward the door unnoticed and unaided. His wife wants to call out but her voice seems to be frozen. She hears a crash and she immediately understands that her husband has gone down.

She cannot see Will anymore as he has approached the hallway. She hears Will call out, *Help me; I fell down.* Then she hears another voice saying, *I can't help you.* Then, there are instructions from someone seemingly in charge to get an aide to help Will to his feet.

Will's wife pounds on the double doors and someone comes to open them immediately. She is appalled to see a nurse standing by the medication chart, with Will still on the floor. There is no room for composure as Will's wife lashes out at the nurse who refused to go to Will's assistance.

Momentarily, two aides come to help Will back to his feet and they accompany him to his seat in the dining room while Will's wife asks to speak with someone in charge. The Assistant Director of Nursing comes and the two women go outside the unit to process what had just happened.

Will's wife continues to express her outrage at the actions of staff ignoring Will, allowing him to put himself in danger. The Assistant Director of Nursing listens and says very little. She knows where blame lies and she is not able to refute a direct observation, even an auditory observation.

That evening, the Assistant Director of Nursing calls Will's wife and tells her that the facility was at fault and steps have been made to correct the negligence. She is apologetic and she makes no excuses for the wrongs done to Will that day.

Will's wife is now more settled. When the Assistant Director of Nursing then asks if Will's wife wants the written incident report to go to the State reporting agency, Will's wife graciously says no. But, she does ask if maybe Will should be left in his wheelchair during the noon meal.

Perhaps, she thinks aloud, **Will only remembers not to rise when he is in the wheelchair.** But, she knows that is incorrect as Will has fallen on several occasions when in the wheelchair. The Assistant Director of Nursing explains they must always attempt the least restrictive approach when residents fail. That is why staff placed Will in a regular chair during lunch. It was a measure of attempting to allow maximum freedom.

Will's wife begins to visualize the problems she had experienced with Will while he remained at home and she nods her understanding of the staff dilemma. Will had falls at home as well. The women talk over the use of a chair alarm and Will's wife agrees to that.

The following day, Will's wife again goes to observe and she sees an orderly unit. No one knows she is there. No one fails to notice the needs of the residents. No one is preoccupied with thoughts other than taking care of those in the House.

She decides to introduce herself to the new Administrator. Will's wife has already been told that the Interim Administrator left after two days at the House. She was obviously not ready to steer a ship caught in a storm.

Corporate then came to attempt to restore administrative order in the House and they apparently did a good enough job until the new ship Captain arrived.

The new Administrator greets Will's wife and thanks her for stopping in. She explains that memory care units are always a challenge as there is a precarious balance between safety versus freedom in nearly every move of every resident. Deterioration can occur in a week, or in a minute.

The Administer explains that needs changed dramatically from one day to the next and staff will then be caught off guard. The Administrator thanks Will's wife for her input and again asks if she wants to formally report the incident. Will's wife smiles and then says, *Had you not asked, I might have.*

Sometimes, the response to an incident is just as critical as the incident itself.

***

"This is the part of life that doesn't sit well with me and never will. It tears my heart in pieces, robs me of gratitude, drains me of anything positive and eats at the faith that holds on. It goes against kindness."
Shannon L. Adler

CHAPTER THIRTY-FIVE
Jerri and Lettie

It is soon apparent to most visitors that even with all the changes in staff, the Memory Care Unit has held intact. It is not because of staff turnover; it is despite that fact.

There are many long-term aides at the House as well as nurses that have devoted years to caring for those with disordered minds and frail bodies. Jerri and Lettie are two such nurses. Without direction, they instinctually know what to do. They know when to hug resident and they understand when to ignore negative behaviors. They know how to direct and they know how to let go of formality and rules in times of crises.

On this day, all has run smoothly until there is a shout down the hall from the nursing station. *No, Victor, no, please.* Jerri is making an entry into the computer but she recognizes the distress in Lettie's voice and she goes scurrying down the hall.

Victor is new to the unit and he is still trying to make sense of his environment. Lettie has met Victor in the hallway with the medication cart and has handed him his cup of medication. She then picks up a paper cup filled with water to hand to Victor. Victor misinterprets Lettie's action and he impulsively smacks his hand on her face, yelling that no one is going to tell him what to do.

Lettie is stunned but she tries to calm Victor with words that only seem to heighten his sense of confusion and anger. His damaged brain is fixed on a misperception. His eyes are filled with rage and he makes a fist and is prepared to deliver it to Lettie's face when Jerri comes up and distracts Victor with a calming voice requesting that Victor please proceed to the dining room where his friends are waiting for him.

Jerri knows full well that she also is a potential target of Victor's confusion. She is prepared to attempt to restrain his arms if necessary, but she goes with years of instinct and awareness by attempting to distract the out-of-control resident. Distraction is a time-tested technique made to confuse a patient and distract them from a negative action and it is second-nature response to Jerri.

Victor's rage-filled eyes are still focused on Lettie and he appears to want to finish his altercation. So, Jerri asks an aide to escort victor down the hall. *He's a military man, Casey, and he has a lot of good stories to tell,* Jerri says. She has directed the aide in how to handle the resident by talking about the known. At least, it is a known for Victor at that moment and on that day.

The aide immediately picks up on the direction, asking in what branch of the service Victor had served. The aide offers her hand to Victor and Victor takes his offending hand and puts it into Casey's guiding hand. As they approach the dining room, Jerri puts her arm around Lettie and says it is time to go to the family room.

Lettie wheels her cart up the hallway and places it behind the nursing station and the two nurses proceed into the family room, closing the door behind them. No one can do anything to help them. Only the Old Guard of nurses know what to do. They must let go, and they must let go immediately. There is work to be done.

Jerri takes a paper towel from the sink, wets it and places the cool cloth on Lettie's red cheek. Then, she wipes the tear streaking down Lettie's other cheek. Jerri says, **He's new** and Lettie says, **I know.** And, it is done. Both women return to the station and finish out their shifts without another word. Last week when Andrew had gotten out of control, it hadn't gone quite so smoothly. Both nurses felt they got off *lucky* this time.

This scene repeats itself several times a week. Most people simply would not put up with it. But, fortunately for those in the house of final release, most facilities have a Jerri or a Letti and that's how they get through the expected staff turnovers and the multiple deaths and the scathing comments from visitors. They are the glue.

Both Charlie's wife and Will's wife have witnessed staff being disrespected and attacked. Charlie's wife thinks it takes a special kind of individual to look past the disordered mind to the core of an individual who has already been stripped of most of his/her basic respect. Will's wife thinks that people like Lettie and Jerri are miracle-workers. But, when she thinks again, she thinks that some probably need more training because they do make mistakes. When she follows up that thought, she concludes that still others are misplaced in their jobs. It's a little like a biological family, she concludes. Everyone needs to adjust as needs change and, lots of mistakes are made along the way.

In any memory care unit, there are aides and nurses who routinely and methodically deliver care with respect and compassion, even when they are met with abuse and disrespect. They are made of something different than most of us.

***

"I want to live the rest of my life, however long or short, with as much sweetness as I can decently manage, loving all the people I love, and doing as much as I can of the work I still have to do."
Audre Lorde

CHAPTER THIRTY-SIX
When All Else Fails

No one in the house of final release ever planned to leave life being cared for in body and mind. For all of them, long-term care was the final option when all else has failed.

Some of those in memory care will remain for days and others, for years. The decision to place a loved one is not taken lightly. Nor, should it be a decision based on guilt and grief.

Children with learning disabilities and/or physical disabilities require specialized education and care. It is no different with those experiencing progressive dementia. But, there is a distinct difference between the child born with a disability and those who have lived progressive lives and are compromised in their golden years. It is cruel to have known a husband, a wife, a parent or any family member as vibrant and productive, only to see them gradually lose the ability to interact effectively with their world. We remember all the wonderful times and all the learning they provided to us personally. We cannot help but want that person until the last moments of their lives.

The time is approaching when that may be a possibility, but we living in this time must deal with the fact that we cannot have what we want. If we give up the idea of what a person *was* and learn honestly what they *are*, we may find a growth curve for ourselves that we never anticipated.

That said, we must be realistic and know when to let go in order to preserve the dignity and safety of our loved ones. If we as family members can no longer serve as a safe community for a loved one, there are specialized facilities with people trained and dedicated to doing just that.

We have all heard horror stories of the old nursing facilities where people moan and shout out and go unattended. If that is an image stopping you from seeking appropriate help for a loved one, you to step back and begin to define basic needs of your loved one and how best they are met. Modern skilled nursing facilities with specialized Memory Care Units are a far cry from outdated images of mass abuse and neglect.

If we hesitate to find appropriate alternative communities for our loved ones because of pressures from those not having such responsibilities, we must remember that advice is easy for those not having to make such a choice.

If we make promises from well-intentioned but misguided feelings of staying the course "until death do us part," we must consider the conditions under which those promises were made. We were young, and we were capable. We and our loved ones grew in ways that could not be anticipated when we made promises with little experience of life.

We must not wait until all else fails. If we wait too long to place loved ones in a community not of our making, we, as caregivers, may be the ones to fail. And, if we know one common thing, it is that our loved ones would never, ever have wanted to put us in a position where we grew so weary and so weak that we, personally would risk failure in our caregiving roles.

Each of us has talents and those talents may or may not include caregiving. We must not wait until we feel helpless or exhausted or bitter. Love does not mean never having to relinquish care. Love means cherishing those we love to the end – in whatever place best suites their needs.

The house of final release is a safe place for people who are cognitively broken and emotionally dismembered. In the House, the flies will continue to hit the fan. With proper training by staff and a consistent attitude of love and compassion by all, those caught in the blades of the fan may grow to feel secure in the knowledge that in this House, the frogs will not have a feast.

Frequently Asked Questions

Reader: Is it not always better to have a loved one remain at home to be cared for by family?

Author: There are many reasons why long-term residential care may be a good alternative for both the dementia patient and the caregiver. One concern is the caregiver's health. About 60% of caregivers of patients with progressive dementia die before the patient. The stress of caregiving someone who does not appropriately comprehend the world is enormous

Secondly, the health of the patient may be better served in a setting in which routine physical and mental health care is available 24/7.

Financially, having 24/7 ongoing health care service at home may be as financially draining than monthly care charges in a memory care facility. Furthermore, crises intervention will be available at the facility. Most memory care units now accept Medicare and Medicaid.

Eventually, outside help will be required not only for the loved one, but for household upkeep. The caregiver will be pulled away from almost all contact with the immediate environment should s/he choose to become the sole caregiver. It is this need to be sole caregiver out of honor or duty that often leads to the demise of the caregiver. In the end stage of the disease, very few progressive dementia patients even know their caregiver(s). It is the stability of the immediate environment, along with opportunities for social stimulation that best serves the need of the patient.

Lastly, the companionship offered at a memory care center is invaluable to a patient who has little comprehension of the current world. In such a facility, everyone struggles to interpret the environment and this affords a commonality of opportunity for interaction which may not be available at home. In addition, patients in a memory care facility are not continually reminded of the deficiency of their cognitions. Staff will respond per the individual patient's need. This need is not dependent upon expressing the need in an appropriate manner as may be the case in a home setting.

Reader: Isn't abuse much more prevalent in a long-term facility than at home where the patient is known and loved?

Author: Logic would dictate that conclusion but you might be surprised to learn that over 60% of abuse is perpetrated by family members. Even home-care healthcare workers are now being caught abusing and neglecting those in their care. Many families are now using home security cameras. Even the best of caregivers cannot avoid the tremendous strain that accompanies care of the progressive dementia patient. Patience is worn thin by days and months and years of caregiving and it just takes a single moment of loss of control for a patient to be abused. Furthermore, no family member is going to report him/herself to authorities for abusing another family member. Thus, the incidence report for family caregivers is no doubt highly underestimated. And it is likely that once abuse begins in the home, it will not only continue; it will escalate.

Abuse comes in the form of emotional, cognitive, physical and financial abuse. And, of course there is also neglect of the needy patient which is also a form of abuse. Yelling, disrespectful language, shoving, hitting and degrading comments are, unfortunately, not atypical. There is a need for caregivers to vent their frustrations and sometimes, the anger is directed toward the patient.

Long term care facilities now have strict state and federal guidelines. Any abuse must be reported and that information is a public record, available for all to read. When abuse occurs in such a facility, the facility has sanctions and the facility is then more closely monitored.

In my years working in long term care facilities, I witnessed numerous incidences of staff being abused by residents. There are such incidences in this book. Only once did I hear a staff member speak disrespectfully to a patient and it was immediately reported to administration. The staff member underwent training in how to better handle the situation. That said, abuse does occur in long term care facilities and it must always be brought to the attention of those able to monitor, train and sanction.

Reader: How can you stay connected to someone you love who has progressive dementia? I mean, it seems impossible to try to relate to them when they just aren't "with it."

Author: The fact that you asked tells me you care about your loved one. As strange as it may seem, you must go where they are and relate to their current interpretations of the world.

Reader: But, isn't that just feeding into a delusional system? That seems disrespectful to me.

Author: Yes, on the surface, it does. But, you must remember, it is that delusional system that tells you where your loved one is *right now*. Your loved one is not capable of being "brought back" to reality because her/his reality is warped and not available due to damaged brain processing.

There is no disrespect is jumping into a scenario and asking questions. Answers to those questions may well be emotional gifts of connection which can keep you bonded to your loved one. I often did that with my husband while he was still at home and that kind of bonding continued when he went to a memory care facility.

Example: My husband might tell me that he led a group discussion in day care that day. Granted, he was a group member, but if he felt he facilitated the group rather than participated in it, what is the harm? When talking about the group, he felt proud of his verbal skills and he felt part of a meaningful conversation. Later, when in memory care, he told me he was undercover for the Navy. He was giving me valuable information about his current time frame and he spoke with pride and awe that he had been entrusted with such an important duty. Why would anyone want to take away that momentary pleasure? As a bonus, he advised me he no longer had any current-time awareness and that was important information to pass along to the staff. Oftentimes, my husband would be referred to at either "Lieutenant" or as "Doc." It always produced a smile from my husband and it clued me into the fact that he was back in time on that day.

Reader: So, if you are the primary caregiver, how do you stimulate your loved one?

Author: Caregivers must keep in mind that their loved one's stimulation may not be stimulating to the caregiver – and vice-versa. If you feel the need to get out where you feel validated or reinforced, you may want to go it alone or with a friend. A shopping trip may be exhausting for your loved one. Progressive dementia almost always affects the motor strip in the frontal lobe of the brain. Movements are exhausting for many patients. But, movement should be encouraged. Playing balloon volleyball or chair dancing can be rewarding activities for those with limited motor abilities.

You may find solace in attending a church service. But, your loved one may feel out of place due to lack of understanding of what is being said. Music can be a common bond but concerts, plays and movies may be too challenging. I loved to sit at home, put in a classical music CD and sit outside where my husband could simply listen and view the garden while each of us gave our own unique interpretations to the music.

Reader: I'm not sure how to ask this but, isn't it just plain wrong to lock up people? I mean, you say the memory care units are "secure" but that's just another way to say people are locked up.

Author: When you think about it, most of us are restrained for a good portion of our lives. Infants experience many restraints for their safety. They are not cognitively compromised but they are vulnerable to engaging in acts which could severely harm them because they do not yet understand cause and effect. And so, we go where they are – to the needs they display at that point in time.

Young children must have rules and regulations as a teaching measure as well as for their safety and well-being. It is a learning process which shapes them to various expectations for cognitive, emotional, behavioral and social success.

Young adults are frequently limited or confined in their dreams by financial and experiential bonds. They simply do not have life experience or financial resources to be able to carry through with many of their own desires. And, in middle adulthood, there are obligations of family and career which constrain many from doing as they truly wish.

When you conceptualize the life experience of dementia patients, they are not so different from other elderly adults who learn from clues that some things simply are not available to them. When someone bangs on the door to get out of a secured unit, a friendly aide leading them back to the group room acclimates them to expectations in the memory care unit. Soon, it is not a problem that the door is locked because safety and desired interaction is contained within the unit.

Reader: How do you know you have a good placement for your loved one?

Author: That's probably the most critical question of all. You need to research and visit. As difficult as it is to visualize your loved one being cared for by others, there must be a good match of personality to setting. In this book, Charlie's wife was impressed that staff knew the names of residents. You cannot imagine how important that single issue may be. In the end stages of dementia, a name may be all that is remembered by the resident. It is a personal greeting that secures a patient to the new caregivers.

But, beyond that, each care provider in a long-term care facility should have background on the patient. Care-giving behaviors may seem invasive or embarrassing for the patient. But, if the care provider can talk about a past career, a grandchild or years in military service during care duties, a feeling of safety and trust occurs.

You may want to go to facilities at different times of the day and on different days. You are looking for continuity of care. You are *not* looking for elegant appointments. Those are things that make *you* comfortable. Chances are, your loved one has not noticed those pleasing environmental settings. Of course, it is different in an assisted living setting where appointments may serve to make a resident feel at home. But, with progressive dementia patients, care level is the most important.

If a facility has staff who have been in their positions for years, that is a good sign. You might ask about reviews from peers, directors or families of past residents. But, as illustrated in the book, all facilities have turnovers and sometimes, they come in multiples. In the book examples, the nurses and aides provided stability when major turnover were experienced in the House. From time to time, any facility *must* have turnovers, as staff members are subject to aging issues as well.

Reader: I find it difficult to talk with someone who can't effectively talk with me. It is just so awkward.

Author: There are many forms of communication. A joint coloring book activity can be relaxing while you bring your loved one up to date on your own life. No response is necessary. Avoid phrases such as "Do you remember...." and "Remember when...." Simply tell your story. If you ask open-ended questions, be prepared for silence. As the dementia progresses, it only rarely likely that a loved one will process the information, hold it in short term memory and then, find a passageway in the brain tangles to be able to respond. If you are sitting during lunch, ask about the food.

Use the prompts available to you. Look around and point to things about which the patient may have interest. With my husband, it was the fish tank. So, I cognitively went to where he was and we talked about the fish. We talked about their movement, their coloring, their size and shape and what they might eat. In doing so, I learned that my husband was probably missing the water.

He was a long-term Navy man and so, the next time I visited, I brought in pictures of his Navy years and he talked during the entire visit about his experiences. Your loved one must feel "safe" to disclose thoughts verbally. That is why brain-compromised loved ones will frequently talk more in a day care setting or a memory care unit when they would not talk at home. You and other non-compromised family members were ongoing reminders of what the loved one could no longer process.

Reader: Is there any good reason to get to know the staff of the memory care unit or should your primary focus continue to be on your loved one?

Author: So glad you asked that. It is critical to familiarize yourself with the new care providers. They need to know about your loved one so that they can make a smooth transition for her or him with as little stress as possible. But, beyond that, they are well trained but also prone to stress. Stress can lead to poor judgment.

Sometimes, staff actions must be swift and direct to protect a patient. The more they know about how to respond, the better the outcome. Caregivers in a facility thrive on immediate recognition of a given resident's history and current condition. It is frequently a small bit of information that allows staff to successfully avert confusion, frustration and chaos for the resident.

Care providers in memory care units are subject to ongoing abuse themselves, simply because they are mandated by law to provide the least restrictive environment to those who simply cannot adequately process their world. Although a few are simply getting more experience or biding their time until something better comes along, most care providers are dedicated and courageous people who truly care about quality of life for your loved one.

Again, look to the book. There were numerous care providers who had worked for decades with those that most of us simply could not handle. The small, everyday kindnesses they offered are not mandated by law. They are acts of caring – acts of love.

It is difficult to relinquish one to memory care following years of being a sole caregiver. But, when a loved one is placed, we must respect the expertise of those trained to go the last mile for us. And, we must also think of all the errors in judgment and action we also made as caregivers.

Reader: What is the difference between a nursing home and a memory care unit?

Author: Memory Care Units are specifically designed to help the resident with moderate to severe impaired memory and judgment to feel he or she is in an environment in which there is the opportunity to again view the world as consistent and, to some extent, knowable. The resident grows to understand that help is always available and that demands on their abilities will not exceed current functioning. Residents see themselves as equal to others. They do not experience the ongoing confusion about why their actions appear out of synch with those of the community at large. They gain feelings of safety and efficacy in seeing that expectations equal their ability to perform on any given day.

In a general, skilled nursing facility, care of physical status is the focus of attention. In a Memory Care Unit, staff attends to physical needs but they also have training in how best to assess and accommodate to cognitive deficiencies which may also lead to problems in physical functioning.

About the Author

Dr. Karen Hutchins Pirnot is a licensed Clinical Psychologist who has treated children and their families for decades. While in private practice in Iowa, she worked extensively with the Department of Human Services and the Juvenile Justice System.

After her move to Florida, Dr. Pirnot worked in private private practice and contracted to long term care facilities to assess and treat various forms of dementia.

Many of Dr. Pirnot's book characters are patterned after traits of the children treated in her practice. She stresses instilling a sense of efficacy in children. Adult characters are viewed as resourceful and capable of making life-changing decisions. In the course of becoming an Alzheimer's caregiver, Dr. Pirnot utilized many of the same interventions that help children toward a better quality of life. The author currently resides in Sarasota, Florida with her adult children and her grandchildren.

Other Books by Dr. Pirnot

GENERAL
As I Am
Just a Common Lady
The Learners of Owamboland
Keeper of the Lullabies
Eating Through the Earth
Nothing Left to Burn; A Caregiver's Voice

CHILDREN'S PICTURE BOOKS
The Blue Penguin
A Colorful Day
Rainbows are the Best
Sam's Perfect Plan
The Door in the Floor
Night Traveler
Just Hanging Out
The Colors of Myself
Please Be My Hands

MID-GRADE READERS

Ordinary Kids Series:
Peter, the Pole and the Knob
The Above All Others Principle
Potsie and the Apparition of Brave Wolf
Morgan and Clive
The Days and Nights of Crighton
Immanuel

Skymasters Series:
Galaxy Girl
Under the Universe
Through a Black Hole
The Multiverse
Silky and Sly:
The Ghost of Gasparilla
The Victorian House

To contact Dr. Pirnot **go to:**
www.drpirnotbooks.com

Made in the USA
Lexington, KY
19 May 2017